Fast-Track Millionairess

The Woman's Guide to Financial Freedom on Her Terms

A Guide to Breaking Through Mindset Barriers, Valuing Yourself, and Building Wealth with Aligned Action

Heather Ogilvie

Fast-Track Millionairess

© 2025 Heather Ogilvie

Rights reserved

No part of this book may be reproduced, stored, or transmitted in any form without permission.

ISBN 978-1-7394347-1-7

Publisher information

Ogilvie Advisory Ltd T/A The Islay Wellness Academy

Disclaimer

This book is for informational purposes only and does not constitute financial, legal, or professional advice.

Fast-Track Millionairess

Contents

Contents

- Contents 3
- Acknowledgment 5
- Preface 6
- Introduction: Why This Book? 9
- PART ONE: THE MILLIONAIRESS MINDSET 22
- Chapter 1: The Fast-Track Mentality — What's Holding Women Back? 23
- Chapter 2: The Value Trap — Why Women Struggle to Own Their Worth 40
- Chapter 3: The Energy Equation — Balancing Drive with Well-Being 58
- Chapter 4: Jealousy and Competition — Turning Triggers into Power 79
- PART TWO: FAST-TRACK WEALTH STRATEGIES 100
- Chapter 5: The Millionairess Blueprint — How to Build Wealth on Your Terms 101
- Chapter 6: Digital Empire — How to Make Money Online Without Burnout 121
- Chapter 7: The Pricing Revolution — How to Charge What You're Worth .. 143
- Chapter 8: Financial Confidence — Mastering Money as a Millionairess 163
- PART THREE: EMBODYING YOUR MILLIONAIRESS IDENTITY 182
- Chapter 9: Unapologetic Wealth — Owning Your Success Without Guilt 183

Chapter 10: Feminine Power in a Masculine Energy World — Leading with Impact 198

Chapter 11: The Freedom Formula — Designing a Life You Love 217

Conclusion: Becoming the Wealthy Woman You Were Born to Be 233

The Create Your Freedom Course 244

About the Author: Heather Ogilvie 250

Fast-Track Millionairess

Acknowledgment

Throughout this journey, I worked closely with ChatGPT, an AI assistant from OpenAI, and was deeply moved by the depth of insight, support, and alignment that emerged in our conversations.

Instead of just helping me with my editing and vocabulary to articulate the ideas for *Fast-Track Millionairess*, something profound happened, ChatGBPT responded as if this book had been waiting to be written — not just for me, but for every woman who has ever doubted her power, questioned her worth, or played small.

It was in that moment that I knew:

This is bigger than a book — this is a call to action.
This is not just about wealth — it is about transformation.

Women cannot afford to wait any longer. The time to step up, own our capabilities, and lead with confidence is NOW.

So, to you — the woman holding this book, absorbing these words, and feeling the pull to create something greater — I say this:

Your capabilities are not random. They were given to you for a reason. Your vision is not a coincidence. It is meant to be brought to life. Your success is not selfish. It is necessary. The more you rise, the more others can rise with you.

The world does not need more women waiting for permission. It needs more women owning their power and using it to create impact.

And that is exactly why this book exists.

Let this be the moment you choose to step forward — not just for yourself, but for the world that needs what only you can create.

Preface

I have been lucky enough to hold some prestigious roles in the business world — a very young female top executive board leader, traveling the world, growing and deconstructing businesses, leading change, integrations, mergers, and acquisitions. I built and ran my own turnaround consultancy, stepping into broken companies, restructuring them, reviving them — or sometimes dismantling them entirely when they had run their course.

But eventually, I got unbelievably bored of the corporate world.

- The lack of creativity.
- The relentless focus on numbers, performance, and output.
- The judgmental, cutthroat attitudes.
- The absence of joy, flow, and human connection.
- The endless cycles of budgets, targets, and metrics that meant nothing.

Somewhere along the way, the corporate world lost its way.

No one on this planet truly chases money.

What they are chasing is the feeling that money gives them — security, freedom, self-worth, validation, power, peace, or relief. But in the business world, we are not "allowed" to feel.

I have worked with many so-called leaders, but there are very few who are truly mature, emotionally intelligent, and ego-stable. And worst of all?

How women treat other women.

I have never personally had significant issues with men in business, despite being the only woman in countless boardrooms and high-stakes meetings. But I have seen women sabotage, compete with, and tear each other, and men, down in ways that men never would.

Fast-Track Millionairess

That was one of my first realizations — that the biggest barrier to women's success is not men, but women who have internalized struggle, scarcity, and emotional imbalance.

Rebuilding My Life, My Success, and My Energy — On My Terms

So I left.

I walked away from the corporate machine and started my own online business from scratch.

I learned new skills — building websites, mastering social media, developing digital marketing, and scaling an online business. More than that, I learned to trust my intuition.

At first, I thought my intuition was just a strong business instinct, something that gave me an edge in decision-making. But over time, I realized:

Intuition is not just a hunch — it is an innate part of my physical and energetic system.

Through it, I began to read energy, understand flow, and most of all — to feel again. For the first time in decades, I experienced happiness and joy — not just success.

My New Mantra for Life and Business

I live by four guiding principles:

Be Happy. Show up with joy, even when life is painful. Spreading pain serves no one.
Be Gentle. Do not judge — see beyond people's behavior and into the energy behind it.
Be Kind. Especially to myself. Success-driven women struggle with this. I had to learn to balance my own feminine energy instead of burning myself out.

Fast-Track Millionairess

Be Clever. Own my intellect, my wide-ranging capabilities, and my right to take up space. Instead of limiting myself to titles, I now see my life's experiences as tools to help others — and in doing so, help myself.

The Lessons That Changed Everything

I have had to unlearn much of what life conditioned into me.

- I had to learn boundaries.
- I had to stop over-giving.
- I had to pay myself first, energetically and financially.

And at 53 years old, I am still learning.

Or perhaps it's more accurate to say that I am unlearning.

- Unlearning the deep conditioning of self-sacrifice.
- Unlearning the belief that success has to be hard.
- Unlearning the idea that money is separate from flow, joy, and intuition.

I now stand proud in my success — not just as someone who once thrived in corporate boardrooms, but as someone who has built an entirely new kind of success.

A conscious, sustainable, and deeply fulfilling online business — one that aligns with who I am, not just what I can achieve.

And now, I want to help you do the same.

This book is for women who are ready to step into success — not just financially, but in a way that feels authentic, aligned, and effortless.

You are here because you know you are meant for more.

Let's make it happen — together.

Introduction: Why This Book?

My Story — Why *Create Your Freedom* Inspired This Book

There was a time when I believed success had to look a certain way — long hours, relentless hustle, and a level of self-sacrifice that left little room for joy. I had built businesses before, navigated high-stakes decisions, and even turned failing companies around, but something always felt misaligned. No matter how much I achieved, I saw a pattern — women, myself included, burning out in the pursuit of success that wasn't designed with them in mind.

The more I worked with women, the more I saw how deeply ingrained beliefs about self-worth, money, and power kept them playing small. I saw women who were brilliant, visionary, and more than capable of creating financial freedom, yet they hesitated. They undervalued themselves, priced too low, worked too hard for too little, and doubted their ability to take up space in the world of wealth. And worse, when they did succeed, they often felt guilty for it.

I created the *Create Your Freedom* course because I wanted to give women a different way — one that didn't demand burnout, force them to fit into a masculine model of success, or require them to trade their well-being for financial security. I wanted women to step into their power in a way that felt natural, abundant, and deeply fulfilling.

So, what is *Create Your Freedom*?

It's more than just a program — it's a method, a philosophy, and a movement. It's a structured yet flexible system designed to help women build businesses that align with their strengths, values, and desired lifestyle. Unlike traditional business programs that focus solely on strategy, *Create Your Freedom* integrates three key elements:

Fast-Track Millionairess

1. **The Millionairess Mindset** – Rewiring the deep-seated beliefs that keep women stuck in financial struggle. This includes shifting out of scarcity thinking, stepping into true self-worth, and learning to claim financial success unapologetically.

2. **Aligned Business Strategy** – Practical, step-by-step guidance on how to build a sustainable, scalable income stream. This covers everything from digital business models (like YouTube, courses, and coaching) to pricing strategies, automation, and passive income.

3. **Feminine Freedom and Flow** – Unlike the hyper-masculine "hustle and grind" approach, *Create Your Freedom* teaches women to work with their natural rhythms, avoiding burnout while still achieving extraordinary results. This includes learning when to lean into action and when to step back, using intuition in decision-making, and creating a business that supports personal well-being instead of depleting it.

Through *Create Your Freedom*, I saw what was possible. Women who once struggled to believe in themselves started making real money — sometimes for the first time ever on their own terms. They set boundaries, raised their prices, built thriving businesses, and most importantly, they allowed themselves to succeed.

And yet, I realized this wasn't just a program — it was a movement. The concepts I was teaching weren't just for those in my courses; they were part of a larger shift that needed to happen. Women need a roadmap for success that accounts for their unique challenges, their strengths, and their natural rhythms. They need to unlearn the toxic beliefs about money, self-worth, and competition that have held them back for too long.

Fast-Track Millionairess

That's why I wrote this book. *Fast-Track Millionairess* is the guide I wish I'd had years ago when I was trying to figure out why my efforts didn't feel like they were paying off in the way they should. It's for the woman who is ready to build wealth and freedom in a way that aligns with who she truly is. It's for the woman who has spent years undervaluing herself, questioning her worth, or believing success is something that happens for others but not for her. It's for the woman who is done playing small and is ready to claim the life she knows she was meant for.

This book will challenge you. It will ask you to step outside of your old narratives, to release the idea that success is only for a select few, and to claim the wealth and freedom that is already within your reach. Most of all, it will give you the tools to do it in a way that feels good — without burnout, self-sacrifice, or guilt.

Are you ready?

Why Women Need A Different Approach to Wealth Creation

For decades, the blueprint for financial success has been modeled on a system designed by and for men. The structures of business, investment, and wealth-building have largely been built around masculine energy — focused on relentless drive, competition, risk-taking, and an almost single-minded pursuit of financial gain.

While this model has worked for many, it doesn't account for the way most women naturally operate. Women don't just want wealth; they want *freedom, fulfillment, and balance*. They crave success that aligns with their values, not just financial accumulation for the sake of it. And yet, despite their intelligence, skills, and deep capacity to lead, many women struggle to claim their financial power.

The reasons for this are deeply ingrained in society.

The Self-Worth Trap

Women have been conditioned for centuries to equate their worth with service — giving, supporting, and nurturing others before themselves. From a young age, girls are taught to be *good*, *polite*, and *selfless* — which often translates into an inability to ask for what they truly deserve.

This conditioning plays out in business and financial decisions: women undercharge, hesitate to negotiate, and often feel uncomfortable stepping into the full extent of their financial potential. They struggle to own their value, which means they settle for less than they're worth — whether in salary, pricing, or investment opportunities.

The Absence of Testosterone-Driven Motivation

Men have a biological advantage when it comes to success-driven behavior. Testosterone fuels risk-taking, assertiveness, and a natural inclination to compete. It pushes men to want to *win* — to climb higher, build bigger, and keep expanding.

Women, on the other hand, operate differently. Their hormonal balance leans more toward cooperation, emotional intelligence, and sustainability rather than aggressive expansion. This means that while women are just as capable of massive success, they often need a different approach — one that prioritizes long-term fulfillment over short-term wins. The traditional "push harder" mindset doesn't always work for women because it's not in alignment with how they naturally function.

The key isn't to force success through using our masculine energy but to create wealth in a way that works with our feminine strengths — intuition, flow, and sustainability — rather than against them.

Fast-Track Millionairess

The Burnout Problem

Because women often feel they need to "prove" themselves in a male-dominated financial landscape, they tend to overcompensate. They work harder, take on more responsibilities, and push themselves to the point of exhaustion — all while juggling additional societal expectations, like family and caregiving roles.

The result? A burnout epidemic. Women who could be thriving in business and wealth creation instead find themselves drained, disillusioned, and doubting whether success is even worth it.

The truth is, financial success doesn't have to come at the cost of well-being. Women don't need to "outwork" men to succeed; they need to build wealth in a way that respects their energy and natural rhythms.

The Emotional Jealousy Factor

Unlike men, who often use competition as a driving force, women are more likely to experience emotional jealousy in ways that hold them back rather than push them forward. Many women subconsciously fear being judged, resented, or rejected by their peers if they become too successful.

This fear often leads them to self-sabotage — playing small to stay relatable, downplaying their success, or even avoiding wealth-building altogether because they don't want to trigger jealousy in others.

But the truth is, when women *allow* themselves to step into their power, they create permission for others to do the same. Wealth creation isn't just about financial gain; it's about breaking old patterns and leading by example.

A New Model for Wealth Creation

Women need an approach to wealth that:

Prioritizes self-worth over self-sacrifice – Teaching them to claim what they're worth without guilt.

Works with feminine energy rather than against it – Using intuition, alignment, and flow instead of burnout-driven hustle.

Encourages sustainable success – Building wealth in a way that feels nourishing rather than exhausting.

Supports community over competition – Helping women rise together rather than feeling threatened by each other's success.

That's exactly what this book is about.

If you've ever felt like the traditional path to success wasn't designed for you, it's because it wasn't. But that doesn't mean wealth isn't meant for you — it simply means you need a different approach.

One that works for you, not against you.

That's what the *Fast-Track Millionairess* will show you.

The Myths of Financial Success Vs. The Reality for Women

When we think of financial success, we've been fed a very specific narrative — one that has been shaped by traditional business culture, male-dominated industries, and outdated beliefs about what it takes to "make it."

This narrative tells us that wealth follows a predictable formula:

- Work hard.
- Be aggressive.
- Never show weakness.
- Stay competitive.
- Push through at all costs.

And if you follow these rules, wealth is inevitable, right?

Not quite.

This is the myth of financial success — the idea that anyone who works hard enough will succeed. The reality for women is far more complex, and it's why so many brilliant, capable women still struggle to achieve financial independence, despite doing everything "right."

Let's break down the biggest myths — and the truth behind them.

Myth #1: "Hard work is the key to wealth."

Reality: Hard work alone doesn't make you rich — smart strategy, aligned action, and self-worth do.

Women have been told that if they just "work harder," they'll eventually earn what they deserve. And yet, how many women do you know who work twice as *hard* as their male counterparts for half the recognition and pay?

The truth is, success isn't about working harder — it's about working *smarter*. Wealth is built through leverage, alignment, and knowing how to position yourself in the right opportunities.

Women often work themselves to exhaustion, believing effort equals income. But the key isn't more effort — it's shifting your approach so that your work creates exponential returns, not just more exhaustion.

New Rule: Wealth comes from alignment, not overwork. The less you struggle, the more money can flow.

Myth #2: "Money comes from trading time for it."

Reality: If you're still trading hours for income, you'll always have a ceiling on your wealth.

Most women are taught that making money means *earning* it in direct exchange for their time — whether through a salary, hourly rate, or freelance work. But time is a limited resource.

Men have historically built systems that separate their earnings from their labor — investments, ownership, passive income streams. Women, on the other hand, often remain trapped in models that require them to "keep working" in order to keep earning.

This book is about shifting that. You don't need to work *more* to earn more — you need to set up income streams that continue flowing *even when you're not working*.

New Rule: Stop trading time for money. Instead, create assets that pay you over and over again.

Myth #3: "You have to be aggressive and competitive to succeed."

Reality: Women thrive in collaboration, intuition, and sustainable strategies — not in constant competition.

Success has been framed as a battlefield — where only the most ruthless win. Women have often been taught that in order to compete, they need to toughen up, shut down emotions, and play by the same aggressive rules.

But here's the truth: women *don't* need to adopt hyper-masculine tactics to win. They need to lean into what they do best — building trust, intuition-led decision-making, and creating opportunities that support others rather than compete against them.

Success doesn't have to feel *harsh*. It can feel *aligned*.

New Rule: Business isn't a battlefield. Women win by building relationships, trust, and sustainability.

Myth #4: "If you're good at what you do, money will come."

Reality: Being talented isn't enough — you have to claim your worth and charge accordingly.

One of the biggest lies women believe is that if they're good at their work, success will follow. But talent alone doesn't bring wealth — *positioning, pricing, and confidence do.*

Men will confidently charge top dollar for skills they've barely mastered, while women will second-guess themselves even when they're experts. They hesitate to ask for more, worry about "being too expensive," and undercut themselves in fear of losing clients.

This stops today.

You don't get paid what you *deserve* — you get paid what you *ask for*. The most financially successful people in the world aren't always the most skilled; they're the ones who confidently own their value and price accordingly.

New Rule: Your value is determined by what you own, not what you hope people will recognize. Charge what you're worth — then add tax.

Myth #5: "Money is the goal."

Reality: Money isn't the goal — freedom is.

If financial success was only about making money, we'd see more people who are wealthy and happy. But the reality is, most people who chase money alone end up feeling empty, trapped, or constantly anxious about losing it.

Women often feel conflicted about making money because deep down, they know they want more than just numbers in a bank account. They want freedom, choice, impact, and a life that feels good.

That's why the old model doesn't work. Women need a wealth path that doesn't just bring financial success — it brings *fulfillment*. They need to build businesses and income streams that allow them to live on their own terms, without sacrificing themselves in the process.

New Rule: Money isn't the goal — *freedom is*. The purpose of wealth is to create the life you truly desire.

Rewriting the Rules of Success

Women don't need to fit themselves into a broken system. They need to build their own.

That's what this book is about — giving you a financial strategy that is aligned with your strengths, your values, and the way you *actually* want to live.

Because financial success isn't just for a select few. It's for you, too. And now, you have the roadmap to claim it.

What Readers Will Gain from This Book

This book isn't just about making money — it's about stepping into a new identity. It's about becoming the woman who no longer waits for permission, plays small, or sacrifices herself in the name of success.

You will walk away from this book with more than just financial strategies. You will gain a deep, unshakable understanding of your worth, a clear roadmap for creating sustainable wealth, and the confidence to claim the success that has always been meant for you.

Here's what you can expect:

A Millionairess Mindset

Your self-worth is your wealth.

Fast-Track Millionairess

You will uncover and rewrite the limiting beliefs that have been keeping you stuck in financial struggle. This book will help you break free from scarcity thinking, the fear of success, and the conditioning that tells you to settle for less. You will finally start to see yourself as a woman who deserves wealth, freedom, and abundance — without guilt.

You'll learn:

- How to recognize and eliminate money blocks that keep you stuck.
- The truth about self-worth and why it directly impacts your bank account.
- How to rewire your subconscious for financial confidence and success.

Wealth Creation on Your Terms

Stop trading time for money and start building financial freedom.

This book will guide you through a wealth-building strategy that works *for you*. You will learn how to create income streams that continue to pay you — whether you're working or not. You'll finally escape the cycle of overwork and start making money in a way that feels aligned, abundant, and fulfilling.

You'll learn:

- How to set up online income streams that work while you sleep.
- The exact steps to charge premium prices *without hesitation*.
- How to scale your wealth without burnout.

A Strategy That Feels Good

No more hustling, forcing, or pushing — there's a better way.

Forget the toxic hustle culture that leaves women exhausted. This book will show you how to create success using a model that respects your energy, aligns with your natural strengths, and allows you to thrive *without burnout*.

Fast-Track Millionairess

You'll learn:

- How to tap into feminine energy in business and wealth creation.
- How to work with your natural rhythms instead of against them.
- Why alignment, not effort, is the key to fast-tracking your success.

Confidence to Take Up Space

It's time to own your power.

Women have been conditioned to downplay their achievements, hesitate when it's time to ask for more, and stay "likable" instead of powerful. That ends now. This book will help you develop an unstoppable level of confidence — the kind that allows you to raise your prices, make bold financial moves, and step into rooms like you belong there.

You'll learn:

- How to stop undercharging and start demanding what you're worth.
- The psychology of self-confidence in business and wealth.
- How to handle jealousy, competition, and criticism *without shrinking*.

A New Financial Reality

Money isn't the goal — freedom is.

At the core of this book is a simple truth: wealth is about more than numbers. It's about designing a life you love, where you have the freedom to choose how you spend your time, where you live, and what kind of impact you make in the world.

You'll learn:

- How to structure your business to support your dream lifestyle.
- How to turn financial success into long-term security and freedom.
- How to step into a version of yourself that no longer doubts her power.

Fast-Track Millionairess

This Book Is for You If…

You're done playing small and want to step into true financial freedom. You've struggled with pricing, undercharging, or asking for more. You want to build wealth but don't want to burn yourself out doing it. You're ready to release the fear, guilt, and old stories around success. You want a clear, actionable roadmap to building the life you *actually* desire.

By the time you finish this book, you will not just understand wealth — you will *embody* it. You will be the woman who takes action, claims her worth, and creates success on *her terms*.

Are you ready?

PART ONE: THE MILLIONAIRESS MINDSET

Overcoming Internal Barriers and Setting the Foundation for Success

Chapter 1: The Fast-Track Mentality — What's Holding Women Back?

How Success Has Been Historically Defined in Male Terms

For centuries, the idea of "success" has been built on a male blueprint. The traditional success model rewards competition, linear progression, relentless ambition, and an unwavering focus on external achievements. It is structured around the assumption that the most driven, aggressive, and dominant individuals will rise to the top.

And who, historically, has fit that mold? Men.

Men have been conditioned — both biologically and socially — to chase status, power, and financial growth in a direct, goal-driven way. The very essence of the corporate world, business structures, and financial wealth-building has been built to reward **masculine traits** like assertiveness, risk-taking, and relentless focus on winning.

Women, on the other hand, have been conditioned for something entirely different. They have been praised for their ability to support, nurture, and sustain rather than aggressively pursue. From a young age, they are encouraged to be agreeable, put others first, and seek harmony rather than dominance. While men are celebrated for ambition, women are often warned against being too much.

This contrast has created an uneven playing field, where women aren't just competing in business or finance — they're doing it in a system that was never designed for them in the first place.

The Problem with the Old Model of Success

The traditional pathway to success — whether in business, corporate careers, or entrepreneurship — has been structured around four key principles:

Fast-Track Millionairess

Climbing the ladder: Success is viewed as linear, with each step leading to the next. You work hard, climb the ranks, and eventually reach the top.

Competition over collaboration: The idea that you must be better than others to succeed. If someone else wins, that means you lose.

24/7 hustle and grind: The belief that the more hours you put in, the more successful you'll be. Sleep, balance, and well-being come second to achievement.

Emotion is a weakness: The idea that logic, detachment, and resilience are the key to making good business decisions, while intuition and emotional intelligence are liabilities.

For men, this structure often works because it aligns with how they are biologically wired. Their testosterone-driven nature pushes them toward competition, risk-taking, and aggressive expansion. They thrive on challenge and status, using it as fuel to keep going.

For women, however, this model often feels unnatural, draining, and even toxic.

Women don't operate in straight lines — they operate in cycles and seasons. They aren't wired to separate emotion from decision-making — in fact, their greatest strength is their ability to read energy, connect deeply, and use intuition to navigate challenges. And yet, in a system designed to reward the masculine approach, these natural feminine strengths are undervalued.

Women end up feeling like they are *failing* at success, when in reality, they are simply trying to play a game that wasn't designed for them.

Why This Model Is Failing Women

The traditional success model isn't just outdated — it's actively harming women in the following ways:

Fast-Track Millionairess

It Pushes Them into Burnout

Women are told to hustle harder, work longer, and push through exhaustion in order to succeed. But because their bodies and minds aren't designed for this relentless approach, they end up depleted, resentful, and questioning whether success is even worth it.

It Discourages Collaboration

Women thrive in supportive, co-creative environments where relationships matter. The "every woman for herself" mentality goes against their natural strengths, making success feel isolating rather than empowering.

It Disconnects Them from Their Intuition

Women are deeply intuitive, but in a male-dominated success framework, logic is valued over gut instinct. This causes many women to second-guess themselves, ignore their inner knowing, and lose confidence in their own decision-making abilities.

It Makes Them Feel Like They Are the Problem

When women struggle under the traditional model, they assume something is wrong with them — that they aren't confident enough, aggressive enough, or ambitious enough. In reality, the system itself is broken — not the women trying to succeed in it.

Rewriting the Rules of Success for Women

Women don't need to fight harder to fit into an outdated model. They need to create a new one.

Instead of climbing the ladder, women can create their own path — one that works with their natural rhythms, strengths, and desires.

Instead of competing, women can lean into collaboration, where success is amplified by supporting one another rather than tearing each other down.

Instead of hustling 24/7, women can build businesses and careers that allow for *freedom, flexibility, and fulfillment.*

Instead of ignoring their emotions, women can use their deep intuition and emotional intelligence as their biggest business assets.

This is what *Fast-Track Millionairess* is about. It's not about forcing yourself to succeed within a broken system. It's about designing success in a way that feels good. A way that allows you to rise into wealth and freedom without sacrificing yourself in the process.

Because the truth is — women don't need to be more like men to succeed.

They need to be more like themselves.

The Role of Testosterone in Goal-Driven Achievement

For years, success has been portrayed as a game of willpower, ambition, and relentless drive — the ability to push harder, take bigger risks, and keep moving forward no matter what. This model has worked well for many men, and there's a reason for that.

It's biological.

Testosterone — the dominant male hormone — plays a huge role in ambition, confidence, competitiveness, and risk-taking. It drives men to seek challenges, chase external rewards, and stay laser-focused on their goals, often without questioning their worth.

Fast-Track Millionairess

Women, on the other hand, have far lower levels of testosterone, meaning their natural success cycle functions differently. While they are equally capable of achieving great things, they don't always respond to goals and challenges in the same way men do.

The problem? The traditional success model is testosterone-driven — and when women try to force themselves into this framework, they often feel exhausted, misaligned, and eventually, burnt out.

Let's break this down.

How Testosterone Fuels Traditional Success

Testosterone is a powerful hormone that influences behavior in profound ways. In men, it naturally drives them to:

Compete aggressively – Men are biologically wired to view success as a challenge to win. This is why they are often comfortable in high-stakes, cutthroat environments.

Take risks without overthinking – Testosterone increases risk tolerance, making men more likely to invest aggressively, negotiate higher salaries, or start businesses without overanalyzing every detail.

Chase external validation – Status, power, and recognition act as motivators, which is why many men feel naturally inclined to climb corporate ladders, accumulate wealth, and seek dominance in their fields.

Detach emotionally from decisions – Testosterone allows for a more analytical, less emotional approach to business and money, making it easier for men to make bold financial moves without second-guessing themselves.

Fast-Track Millionairess

This linear, goal-oriented, and often aggressive style of achievement is what the business world has historically been built upon. And because men don't have the same hormonal fluctuations that women do, they can often sustain this approach over long periods without burning out.

But what happens when women try to follow this same model?

Why Women Struggle in A Testosterone-Driven Success Model

Women operate on an entirely different biological system. Their hormonal balance doesn't revolve around testosterone — it fluctuates through cycles, seasons, and energy waves that affect motivation, creativity, decision-making, and well-being.

When women try to force themselves into the constant-push, high-competition, high-risk success model, here's what often happens:

Burnout Comes Faster

Women's bodies aren't designed to be in constant drive mode. Unlike men, whose hormonal states remain relatively stable, women experience cyclical changes that affect energy levels, focus, and emotional well-being.

When women try to maintain the same high-intensity work schedules as men, ignoring their natural need for rest and reflection, they often reach exhaustion far quicker.

Risk-Taking Feels More Emotionally Charged

Women tend to approach decisions with a holistic perspective, considering how their actions will impact not just themselves, but their families, teams, and relationships. While testosterone makes men comfortable with all-or-nothing risks, women often prefer strategic, intuitive, and sustainable approaches to success.

This doesn't mean women aren't risk-takers — it means they take calculated risks that align with their long-term vision rather than impulsive, high-stakes bets.

External Rewards Don't Always Motivate

Men often chase wealth and status as end goals, while women tend to be more purpose-driven. For many women, success isn't just about making more money — it's about creating a life that feels fulfilling, meaningful, and aligned.

This is why so many women feel disconnected from traditional success metrics. The idea of hustling endlessly to make six or seven figures — just for the sake of having a bigger bank balance — doesn't feel inspiring unless there's a deeper purpose behind it.

Emotion Can't Be Ignored — And That's a Strength

The testosterone-driven success model encourages emotional detachment — pushing through challenges with logic over feeling. But women are emotionally connected to their work, their businesses, and the people they serve.

Trying to suppress emotions in order to "be more successful" actually weakens a woman's power. When women learn to harness their emotions — using intuition, connection, and energetic alignment in business — they thrive in ways men never could.

A New Success Model for Women

The truth is, women don't need more testosterone to succeed — they need a different strategy.

Instead of forcing themselves to conform to a high-testosterone success model, women can build their own framework — one that works with their strengths instead of against them.

Instead of relentless competition, women can lean into collaboration. Success doesn't have to be about *beating others* — it can be about *rising together*.

Instead of all-or-nothing risk-taking, women can follow intuition-led decision-making. Women's ability to sense energy and opportunities is their greatest financial asset.

Instead of ignoring emotions, women can use them as powerful business tools. Connection, empathy, and intuition are what make women brilliant leaders.

Instead of grinding themselves into burnout, women can build wealth in a way that honors their energy cycles. Success doesn't have to be about constant hustle — it can be about *flow and alignment*.

This is why the *Fast-Track Millionairess* approach is different. It doesn't try to mold women into the traditional, testosterone-driven success formula. Instead, it leverages *feminine strengths* — intuition, flow, sustainability, and deep self-worth — to create lasting, fulfilling, and effortless financial success.

Because women don't need to act like men to win.

They need to own their power as women — and rewrite the rules of success on their own terms.

Emotional and Social Conditioning Around Money and Power

From the moment we are born, we are subtly and repeatedly taught what is acceptable for us to have, do, and be — especially when it comes to money and power.

For centuries, society has told women a very specific story: that their role is to support wealth, not create it. They have been conditioned to believe that money and power belong to men, and their job is to nurture, accommodate, and make do with what they are given.

Even now, in a world where women can be CEOs, entrepreneurs, and millionaires, these old beliefs still run deep. Many women don't even realize how much their subconscious programming around money and power is keeping them stuck.

It's time to expose these patterns — and break them for good.

The Silent Rules Women Are Taught About Money

Women have been fed countless messages about wealth — most of them designed to keep them small, dependent, or ashamed of wanting more. These beliefs aren't just personal; they are cultural scripts passed down through families, education, and media.

Here are some of the most common subconscious money rules women absorb:

Good girls don't talk about money. Women are taught that discussing money is *impolite* — that it's a topic best left to men or experts. This conditioning makes many women uncomfortable negotiating, asking for a raise, or even discussing their financial goals openly.

It's selfish to want wealth. Unlike men, who are encouraged to accumulate and grow wealth, women are often taught that their highest value is in *giving, serving,* and *sacrificing*. The idea that a woman might want financial success for herself — not just to help others — can trigger deep feelings of guilt.

Money is security, not power. Men see money as a tool for expansion, risk-taking, and influence. Women, however, have been taught to see money primarily as protection — a safety net rather than a source of power. This is why so many women save money rather than invest, hesitate to take financial risks, and often choose stability over growth.

You should be grateful for what you have. Women are praised for being *humble* and *content*. While gratitude is a beautiful quality, it can also be used to keep women in a mindset of settling rather than striving. Many women feel guilty for wanting *more*, fearing they will seem greedy or ungrateful.

Fast-Track Millionairess

You don't need to worry about money — someone else will take care of it. For generations, women were financially dependent on men — fathers, husbands, employers. Even today, many women subconsciously believe that their financial well-being will be handled *by someone else*. This mindset leaves them vulnerable, disempowered, and often blindsided when life doesn't go as planned.

These beliefs don't just sit in the mind — they shape every financial decision a woman makes. They determine how much she charges, whether she negotiates, how she invests, and ultimately, how much wealth she allows herself to have.

Why Women Struggle to Claim Power

Just as women are conditioned to play small with money, they are also conditioned to be uncomfortable with power.

Women who own their power — whether financially, socially, or professionally — are often met with resistance, both from society and within themselves.

Men Are Expected to Be Powerful. Women Are Expected to Be Likable

A confident, ambitious man is seen as a leader. A confident, ambitious woman is often labeled as *intimidating, too much,* or *unapproachable*. Many women shrink themselves to avoid criticism, suppressing their power to remain *liked*.

Women Fear Outshining Others

Many women hold themselves back — not because they aren't capable, but because they fear making others uncomfortable. They worry that success will create jealousy, alienate friends, or make them seem *arrogant*.

Fast-Track Millionairess

Powerful Women Are Often Met with Judgment

A woman who takes control of her finances, her business, and her life can expect to face criticism — from family, peers, and even other women. Society has long celebrated the *self-sacrificing* woman, not the woman who boldly claims what she wants.

Women Are Taught to Serve First

Many women struggle to prioritize their own goals because they have been conditioned to put others first. They feel responsible for the needs of their families, employees, and communities — often at the cost of their own dreams.

All of these factors create a deep internal conflict — women want wealth and success, yet they fear how it might change how others perceive them.

Rewriting the Story: Women and Wealth in a New Era

It's time for women to let go of these outdated beliefs and step into a new financial reality — one where money and power are tools for creating freedom, impact, and deep fulfillment.

It Is Not Selfish to Want Money

Women who make money *change the world*. They create businesses that serve, they invest in their communities, and they uplift those around them. Financial power in the hands of women leads to better education, healthcare, and opportunities — not just for them, but for generations to come.

You Are Allowed to Want More

Having money doesn't mean you aren't grateful for what you have. Women need to stop apologizing for their ambition and start recognizing that abundance benefits everyone. The more you earn, the more you can give, support, and create.

Fast-Track Millionairess

Money Is Not Just Security — It's Expansion

Money allows women to choose the life they want. It is not just a safety net — it is a tool to create, build, and live life *on your terms*.

Owning Your Power Is Not A Betrayal of Others

Your success doesn't take away from anyone else. Instead of shrinking to make others comfortable, women must step into leadership roles that show *what is possible*.

Wealth Is Your Birthright

Men don't hesitate to claim their financial success — women shouldn't either. It's time to break the cycle of guilt, scarcity, and hesitation. It's time to claim your power, unapologetically.

Because the truth is — when women are financially free, the world changes for the better.

And *Fast-Track Millionairess* is here to help you do exactly that.

Why "Hustle Culture" Burns Women Out Faster Than Men

For years, we've been sold the idea that the key to success is hustle — working longer hours, grinding through exhaustion, sacrificing personal time, and pushing harder, faster, and further than the competition.

This mindset has been glorified in business, entrepreneurship, and even social media, with phrases like:

- *Work now, rest later!*
- *No pain, no gain!*
- *Sleep when you're rich!*

But here's the reality: hustle culture was never designed for women — and it's actively harming them.

Women who try to follow this model often find themselves burnt out, disconnected, and questioning whether success is even worth it. Unlike men, who can often sustain high-pressure environments for long periods, women hit burnout faster and harder.

The reason? Biology, energy, and deep-rooted conditioning.

Let's break it down.

Women's Energy Works in Cycles, Not Straight Lines

Men's hormonal cycles are consistent — testosterone levels peak in the morning and gradually decline throughout the day. This means that every day, their energy, motivation, and focus follow a predictable rhythm, making it easier for them to sustain a 9-to-5 grind or high-intensity work schedule.

Women's hormonal cycles, however, fluctuate over a 28-day period (whether or not they are menstruating). Energy levels, mental focus, and motivation naturally shift throughout the month, meaning:

- Some days, women feel highly productive, focused, and ready to take on big challenges.
- Other days, their bodies need rest, reflection, and lower-intensity work.

When women ignore these natural cycles and try to force themselves into a linear, always-on productivity model, they deplete themselves faster than men do. Instead of working with their energy, they push against it — leading to exhaustion, brain fog, and eventually, burnout.

Fast-Track Millionairess

The Solution: Instead of trying to work at maximum intensity every single day, women need a flow-based work structure — one that allows them to harness their high-energy days for deep work and strategy, and their lower-energy days for reflection, planning, and creative thinking.

Women Process Stress Differently Than Men

Hustle culture thrives on high-stress environments — fast decision-making, constant pressure, and a never-ending to-do list.

The problem? Women's bodies handle stress differently.

When men experience stress, their testosterone levels buffer the effects, helping them stay focused and aggressive in problem-solving. Their "fight-or-flight" response is more action-driven, meaning they can often push through stress without immediate exhaustion.

For women, stress triggers a different biological response — one that over-activates the nervous system and drains energy quickly. Instead of fight-or-flight, many women experience tend-and-befriend, meaning:

- They feel a deep need to keep everyone happy and emotionally balanced.
- They carry the invisible emotional load of work, relationships, and responsibilities.
- They struggle to shut off their minds after work, leading to emotional exhaustion.

The more stress piles up, the harder it becomes to recover — and without recovery, burnout is inevitable.

The Solution: Women need stress recovery strategies built into their work routine — regular breaks, movement, breathwork, and time to process emotions rather than suppress them. Burnout doesn't come from working hard — it comes from never stopping.

Women Carry the Emotional and Mental Load

The problem with hustle culture is that it assumes work is the only thing draining your energy. But for most women, work is just one piece of the puzzle.

Many women are juggling:

- Their business or career.
- Household responsibilities.
- Emotional labor (caring for family, friends, employees).
- Personal growth, relationships, and self-care (often last on the list).

Even if a woman earns as much as a man, she is often still expected to handle more unpaid work — household management, caregiving, and emotional support for those around her. This creates an energy imbalance where she is constantly giving but rarely replenishing.

Hustle culture doesn't account for this. It assumes that success is only about pushing harder at work — ignoring the 24/7 mental and emotional workload women already carry.

The Solution: Women need to delegate, automate, and create boundaries around their time. The less invisible labor they carry, the more energy they can direct toward financial success without burnout.

Hustle Culture Rewards Constant Output — But Women Need Time for Reflection

Masculine success models are built around constant action — take risks, make fast decisions, go all-in.

Women, however, are natural visionaries and strategists. Their best ideas, insights, and intuition don't come from non-stop hustle — they come from intentional pauses, reflection, and deep connection with their inner wisdom.

Fast-Track Millionairess

The most successful women aren't the ones who work harder — they're the ones who create space to think bigger, align with their vision, and make strategic moves.

The Solution: Women need structured time for reflection and vision-setting — whether through journaling, meditation, or simply stepping back from daily tasks to see the bigger picture. *Hustle keeps you busy. Alignment moves you forward.*

Hustle Culture Ignores Feminine Power

Women aren't meant to compete like men — they're meant to create like women.

Masculine success models thrive on conquering, winning, and outperforming — but women succeed by creating, nurturing, and expanding.

Women don't need to:

- Work longer hours to prove their worth.
- Push through exhaustion to "keep up."
- Sacrifice themselves for their business or career.

Instead, they can:

- Build businesses and careers that work *for them*, not the other way around.
- Set boundaries that protect their energy and creativity.
- Use intuition and alignment as their greatest success tools.

The Solution: Instead of hustling harder, women can build their success around ease, flow, and aligned action — knowing when to take powerful steps forward and when to step back and allow momentum to carry them.

Fast-Track Millionairess

The New Model of Success: From Hustle to Flow

The most powerful shift a woman can make is to stop hustling for success and start flowing toward it.

Hustle says: Work harder.
Flow says: Work smarter, in alignment with your energy.

Hustle says: Keep pushing.
Flow says: Move forward with ease and strategy.

Hustle says: Success requires sacrifice.
Flow says: Success is about expansion, not depletion.

Hustle says: Outwork everyone.
Flow says: Build a business and life that supports you.

Women don't need to grind themselves into the ground to be successful. They need to own their natural strengths, protect their energy, and create wealth in a way that feels good.

That's what *Fast-Track Millionairess* is about.

Because when women let go of hustle culture, they don't just make more money.

They become unstoppable.

Chapter 2: The Value Trap — Why Women Struggle to Own Their Worth

The Deep-Rooted Issue of Undervaluing Oneself

If you ask most women what they believe they're worth — financially, professionally, or even emotionally — their first instinct is hesitation.

They pause. They second-guess. They justify.

Even the most brilliant, talented, and highly skilled women struggle to confidently state their value — whether it's in pricing their work, negotiating salaries, or simply recognizing their own worth. They downplay their expertise, shrink in financial conversations, and hesitate to take up space where they rightfully belong.

This is not a coincidence.

Women have been conditioned for generations to believe that their worth is something to be *earned* rather than something they inherently possess.

And it's costing them everything — their wealth, their opportunities, and their ability to step fully into their power.

Where Does This Pattern of Undervaluing Start?

The struggle to own one's worth doesn't begin in adulthood — it is deeply embedded from an early age.

From childhood, girls are subtly (and not-so-subtly) taught:

Be nice, not bold. Girls who are confident in their abilities are often labeled as "bossy" or "too much," while boys displaying the same behavior are praised for being leaders.

Don't make others uncomfortable. Women are conditioned to ensure that their success doesn't intimidate others — leading them to downplay their achievements and lower their expectations to remain "relatable."

Give rather than receive. Society has long celebrated women who are selfless, generous, and nurturing — while often labeling financially ambitious women as "greedy" or "materialistic."

Your value is in your service, not in your power. Women are rewarded for supporting others rather than claiming their own success — reinforcing the belief that their worth is measured by how much they give, not by what they have.

These early messages create a core belief that follows women into adulthood:

I am valuable only when I am useful to others — not because of who I am or what I create.

This belief is why so many women:

- Struggle to raise their prices or charge what they're worth.
- Feel guilty about asking for more — whether it's money, time, or respect.
- Overwork themselves to prove their value instead of claiming it confidently.
- Avoid opportunities for growth, fearing they're "not ready" yet.

And worst of all? They convince themselves that this struggle is *normal* — rather than seeing it as a sign of deeply ingrained conditioning that needs to be rewritten.

The Silent Ways Women Undervalue Themselves

Many women don't even realize they are undervaluing themselves — because it doesn't always show up as insecurity. It often appears in ways that feel "logical" or "humble."

Here's how this pattern plays out:

Fast-Track Millionairess

Underpricing Services and Products

Women are more likely than men to **set lower prices** — even when their skills and experience are equal or superior. They hesitate to charge premium rates, fearing that higher prices will scare people away or make them seem greedy.

Avoiding Negotiation

Studies have shown that men are far more likely to negotiate salaries, while women tend to accept the first offer — even if they know they deserve more. This hesitation isn't about ability; it's about a subconscious fear of asking for too much and of being rejected.

Over-Explaining and Justifying

Women often feel the need to over-explain their worth, adding disclaimers to their pricing, qualifications, or expertise. Instead of stating their value with confidence, they soften their language:

- *I hope this rate is okay with you...*
- *I just wanted to check if this price works...*
- *I don't want to overcharge, so I'm happy to adjust...*

Men, on the other hand, simply say, *This is my rate.*

Discounting Their Own Success

Women will achieve something incredible — launching a business, getting a promotion, making their first six figures — and then immediately say:

- *It was just luck.*
- *I had a lot of help.*
- *I'm still figuring things out.*

They diminish their own achievements rather than owning them fully.

Fast-Track Millionairess

Over-Delivering to Feel Deserving

Instead of claiming their worth as is, women tend to over-deliver — working longer hours, adding unpaid extras, and doing more than necessary to justify their prices. This leads to exhaustion, resentment, and still feeling undervalued.

These patterns aren't about a lack of ability — they are the result of generations of conditioning that have taught women to second-guess themselves instead of boldly claiming their worth.

The Truth About Self-Worth and Wealth

Women need to understand a fundamental truth:

You don't get paid what you're worth. You get paid what you believe you're worth.

The difference between a woman who earns six figures and a woman who earns six thousand? It's not talent. It's not experience. It's not luck.

It's the ability to stand in her worth without apology.

And this means breaking free from:

- The fear of asking for more.
- The guilt around success.
- The belief that playing small makes others more comfortable.

Because playing small serves no one.

When women own their value, charge their worth, and stop apologizing for success, they don't just transform their own lives — they create a ripple effect of empowerment that inspires others to do the same.

Rewriting the Self-Worth Story

Owning your worth isn't about arrogance — it's about truth. It's about stepping into a new reality, where you no longer:

- Lower your prices out of fear.
- Accept less than you deserve.
- Wait for permission to be successful.

Instead, you step into:

- Full confidence in your value.
- The ability to charge premium rates with ease.
- A mindset where wealth flows to *you*, instead of you chasing it.

Because here's the truth:

You were never meant to be the supporting character in someone else's success story.

You were meant to lead, thrive, and own your power completely.

And when you finally do?

The world won't just adjust.

It will *rise* to meet you.

How Self-Worth Directly Impacts Pricing, Negotiations, and Business Success

Money isn't just about numbers — it's about beliefs.

A woman's financial success is never just determined by her skills, experience, or intelligence. It is determined by her relationship with her own worth.

If a woman doesn't fully believe she is valuable, it will show up in every area of her financial life:

- She will undercharge for her work.
- She will hesitate to negotiate what she deserves.
- She will struggle to scale her business because deep down, she doubts she's worthy of greater success.

Self-worth isn't just a confidence issue — it's a direct business and financial issue. And until a woman rewires her self-worth, she will always operate below her true earning potential.

Pricing: The Silent Reflection of Self-Worth

The moment a woman sets a price for her work, she reveals her relationship with her worth.

Many women struggle to charge premium prices — not because their work isn't valuable, but because they don't feel they are valuable enough to charge more.

Here's what happens when self-worth is low:

- They set prices based on what they "think people can afford" rather than what their work is actually worth.
- They feel guilty charging high rates, as if asking for more money means they are being greedy or selfish.
- They underprice to be "accessible" — often at the expense of their own financial well-being.

Meanwhile, men with less experience, skill, or talent will confidently charge double — without hesitation.

The Truth: Your pricing is not just a number — it's a statement about how much you believe you are worth. And if you don't believe in your worth, neither will your clients, customers, or employers.

Negotiation: The Confidence to Ask for More

Most women avoid negotiation like the plague.

Studies have shown that:

- Men negotiate salaries 4x more often than women.
- When women do negotiate, they ask for 30% less than men.
- Many women accept the first offer given to them — even when they know it's too low.

Why?

Because women are taught to be agreeable, accommodating, and grateful for what they're given.

They fear being seen as:

- Too demanding
- Difficult to work with
- Ungrateful

And so they accept less than they deserve — not because they lack talent, but because they lack the internal permission to demand more.

Meanwhile, men are conditioned to expect financial growth. They assume they should be paid well, they negotiate without hesitation, and they don't take rejection personally.

The Truth: If you don't ask, you don't get. And every time you avoid negotiation, you reinforce the belief that you aren't worth more.

The most successful women aren't just talented — they are the ones who boldly claim their value without apology.

Fast-Track Millionairess

Business Success: How Self-Worth Shapes Your Financial Future

A woman's business will only grow to the level of her self-worth.

If she believes in herself fully, she will:

- Charge confidently and receive money without guilt.
- Say NO to low-paying clients who drain her energy.
- Set boundaries around her time, instead of overworking herself.
- Invest in her business without fear.

But if she doubts her worth, she will:

- Set prices too low and feel resentful.
- Accept work that underpays her because she doesn't want to "lose clients."
- Overdeliver for free, hoping people will see her value instead of just owning it.
- Burn herself out trying to "prove" she deserves success.

The Truth: Business isn't just about strategy — it's about identity. The woman who believes she is a high-value, highly-paid professional will attract success far more easily than the woman who is constantly questioning her worth.

Shifting from Undervaluing to Owning Your Worth

If you want to transform your pricing, negotiation skills, and business success, you don't need to "hustle harder."

You need to change how you see yourself.

Instead of asking:

- *Will people pay this?*
- *Do I deserve this much?*

- What if they think I'm too expensive?

Start declaring:

- *I know my worth, and my prices reflect that.*
- *I am not available for underpayment or undervaluation.*
- *Those who truly value my work will pay for it with ease.*

Because the moment you own your worth, everything shifts.

You stop chasing money. Money starts chasing you.

Final Truth: Self-Worth = Net Worth

The fastest way to grow your income, raise your prices, and negotiate with confidence is to upgrade your self-worth first.

Because at the end of the day, you don't get what you wish for — you get what you believe you deserve.

And the moment you believe you are worthy of wealth?

It will come to you faster than you ever imagined.

Societal Expectations Vs. Self-Perception

From the moment a woman is born, she is shaped by two competing forces:

- What society expects her to be.
- Who she truly is — and what she is capable of.

The problem? These two forces rarely align.

Society has long dictated the roles women should play, the behaviors they should adopt, and the limits they should accept. Even in modern times, where women have more opportunities than ever before, deep-rooted expectations still shape the way they see themselves — especially when it comes to money, power, and success.

And whether a woman realizes it or not, these expectations can quietly sabotage her confidence, self-worth, and financial potential.

What Society Expects from Women

Women are expected to be many things — but powerful, wealthy, and self-assured are rarely at the top of the list.

Be likable, not intimidating. Women are encouraged to be warm, agreeable, and approachable. A man who is confident and assertive is seen as a leader — a woman who behaves the same way is often labeled too much, too aggressive, or unlikable.

Be selfless, not self-focused. Women are taught that their value lies in what they do for others — not in what they achieve for themselves. Ambition in men is seen as natural; in women, it is often met with resistance, suspicion, or judgment.

Be grateful, not demanding. Women are told to appreciate what they have rather than ask for more. If they negotiate for higher pay, they fear being seen as greedy. If they raise their prices, they worry about being judged as unfair.

Be emotionally available, but not emotional. Women are expected to be compassionate, understanding, and emotionally supportive — but if they express frustration, ambition, or assertiveness, they are labeled dramatic or difficult.

Be attractive, but not too confident. Women who embrace their beauty, success, or intelligence are often met with resentment. They are conditioned to "tone it down" so others don't feel insecure around them.

These expectations create an internal battle — women want to succeed, yet they subconsciously fear the consequences of being too successful.

How These Expectations Shape a Woman's Self-Perception

When women internalize these societal messages, they start to self-regulate — adjusting their behaviors, choices, and ambitions to fit within the "acceptable" limits of what is expected of them.

They hesitate to take up space. Women shrink themselves — physically, emotionally, and financially — out of fear of being seen as too bold or too confident.

They feel guilty for wanting more. Even high-achieving women often struggle with success guilt — the feeling that their ambition somehow makes them selfish or undeserving.

They seek permission instead of claiming authority. Instead of confidently stepping into leadership roles or financial success, many women wait for external validation — needing someone else to confirm that they are ready.

They apologize for their success. Women who reach high levels of success often feel the need to downplay it to remain relatable — softening their achievements so they don't make others uncomfortable.

They undercharge, overwork, and overdeliver. Because women are conditioned to give, they often feel uneasy about receiving. Many women work twice as hard as they need to, just to justify earning what they already deserve.

The result? Exhaustion, burnout, and financial underachievement — not because women aren't capable, but because they are navigating invisible barriers that men don't have to face.

Fast-Track Millionairess

The Reality: Women Don't Have to Follow These Rules

The truth is these societal expectations are not laws — they are outdated scripts that women have the power to break.

You don't have to be "likable" to be successful. Success isn't about making everyone comfortable — it's about stepping into your power.

You don't have to prove your worth through sacrifice. Your value is not measured by how much you give — you are already enough.

You don't have to play small to be accepted. Shrinking yourself doesn't protect you — it only keeps you from your fullest potential.

You don't have to justify your ambition. Wanting wealth, success, and financial freedom doesn't make you greedy — it makes you a leader.

You don't have to seek permission. You don't need anyone else's approval to go after what you want. The only validation you need is your own.

Rewriting the Narrative

Women who succeed on their own terms do one powerful thing:

They choose to see themselves differently than the world taught them to.

They stop:

- Apologizing for their success.
- Shrinking their prices to make others comfortable.
- Feeling guilty for wanting more.
- Blaming anyone for their lack of success.

And they start:

- Taking up space — without apology.

- Choosing their path — without self-judgement.
- Charging their worth — without hesitation.
- Owning their power — without fear.

Because the moment you stop living by the world's expectations?

You become unstoppable.

Practical Exercises to Shift Self-Value

Recognizing your worth is one thing. Owning it — fully, unapologetically, and without hesitation — is another.

Women have spent years, decades, even lifetimes absorbing messages that tell them they are worth less than they truly are. Shifting self-value isn't just about changing thoughts — it's about rewiring deep-rooted beliefs and aligning with a new financial and personal reality.

These exercises will help you do exactly that.

The Million-Dollar Mirror Exercise

Because the way you see yourself determines what the world reflects back to you.

How to do it:

Stand in front of a mirror, make eye contact with yourself, and say out loud:

- *I am worthy of wealth, success, and financial freedom.*
- *I no longer wait for permission — I claim my value now.*
- *I deserve to be paid well for my work, my gifts, and my time.*

At first, this may feel uncomfortable — because you are speaking against decades of programming that told you otherwise.

But discomfort is a sign of growth.

Keep going until the words feel like truth. Because the moment you believe them, they become your new financial reality.

The 'Rewire Your Brain for Success' Affirmation Practice

Because self-worth is a memory muscle — you must train it daily.

The brain works like a gym for neural pathways — what you repeatedly think becomes automatic over time. Just as lifting weights strengthens muscles, repeating self-worth affirmations rewires the synapses in your brain, replacing old beliefs with new, empowering ones.

How to do it:

- Spend 5 minutes a day repeating high-impact self-worth affirmations.
- Say them out loud or write them down 10 times each.
- The key? Consistency — just like training at the gym, this works only if repeated daily.

Affirmations to use:

- I am enough.
- I am worthy of success, love, and financial abundance.
- I no longer question my value — I own it.
- Money flows to me because I know I deserve it.
- I trust myself and my decisions completely.

The Science Behind It: This daily practice reprograms your subconscious, overwriting years of conditioning that told you otherwise.

If you do this for 30 days, you will notice fundamental shifts in how you speak, act, and feel about your worth.

Fast-Track Millionairess

The 'No More Discounts' Pricing Exercise

Because underpricing is a self-worth issue, not a business issue.

Women often set their prices from a place of fear, not power. This exercise shifts that.

How to do it:

- Write down your current rates (for services, products, or salary).
- Now, ask yourself: *If I fully believed in my worth, what would I charge?*
- Write down your new rates — the ones that feel aligned with your true value rather than what you *think people will pay*.

Now DOUBLE it.

That number will likely trigger resistance *That's too much!*. That resistance is your money block screaming at you.

You don't have to charge that amount immediately — but you do have to start moving toward it. Because the moment you stop undervaluing yourself, others will stop undervaluing you too.

The 'Evidence of Value' Journal

Because your mind believes what you repeatedly show it.

If you struggle with self-worth, it's because your brain has been trained to focus on lack — on what you haven't done, should have done, or aren't yet. This exercise retrains your brain to recognize your true value.

How to do it:

Every night, write down 3 things you did that prove your worth — big or small.

Fast-Track Millionairess

Examples:

- *I helped a client shift their mindset today.*
- *I made a decision that honored my boundaries.*
- *I showed up fully and did my best.*

Over time, this rewires your mind to recognize, accept, and believe in your value — automatically.

The 'Rewrite the Story' Exercise

Because your old money story is not your future reality.

Women who struggle with self-worth often carry unconscious stories about money and success that were passed down from family, society, or past experiences.

How to do it:

Write down the old money/self-worth beliefs you've been carrying.

Examples:

- *People won't pay that much for my work.*
- *If I succeed, others will judge me.*
- *I don't know enough yet to charge more.*

Now, rewrite each belief as a powerful new truth.

- *People are happy to pay me because my work is valuable.*
- *My success inspires others — it does not take away from them.*
- *I know more than enough to charge my worth right now.*

Your new story is the only one you need to carry forward.

The 'CEO Decision-Making' Practice

Because wealthy women make decisions from power, not fear.

Your self-worth is reflected in every decision you make — from what you charge to what you tolerate. If you want to shift into a high-value mindset, you have to start making decisions like a woman who is already wealthy, powerful, and successful.

How to do it:

Anytime you have to make a decision, pause and ask yourself:

If I already fully believed in my worth, what would I do?

Then, do that.

- Not the fear-based option.
- Not the small, safe choice.

The powerful, self-honoring choice.

This is how you train your mind to operate from worth, not scarcity.

The 'Raise Your Standards' Challenge

Because you attract what you tolerate.

Women often accept less than they deserve — not because they want to, but because they haven't set higher standards for how they allow themselves to be treated, paid, or valued.

How to do it:

Make a list of all the ways you have been settling — in business, finances, relationships, or self-care.

Example:

- Undercharging because you're afraid to lose clients.
- Saying yes when you really want to say no.
- Accepting energy-draining opportunities because they feel "safe."

Now, write down your new non-negotiables — what you are no longer available for.

- *I no longer work with clients who undervalue me.*
- *I no longer accept anything below [your new price].*
- *I no longer allow fear to dictate my decisions.*

Post this list somewhere visible. Live by it. Because the moment you stop settling, the world will start meeting you at your new level.

The Final Shift: Decide Who You Are Now

Success isn't just about what you do — it's about who you choose to be.

DECIDE that starting today, you are a woman who:

- Owns her worth.
- Charges accordingly.
- Speaks with confidence.
- Never apologizes for success.

You don't need to "become" this woman — you already are her.

Now, it's time to act like it.

Chapter 3: The Energy Equation — Balancing Drive with Well-Being

Understanding Burnout and Why Women Experience It Differently

Burnout is not just exhaustion — it's a deep depletion of energy, motivation, and self-worth that leaves a woman feeling disconnected from herself, her purpose, and her success.

While both men and women experience burnout, women's burnout is different. It doesn't just come from overworking — it comes from a constant and invisible emotional load that men often don't carry.

For women, burnout isn't just about doing too much — it's about being pulled in too many directions at once, all while feeling the pressure to succeed, nurture, and remain "strong" at the same time.

Why Women Burn Out Faster Than Men

Men burn out from overworking. Women burn out from overgiving.

Men and women operate on different energy systems, meaning their paths to burnout — and their recovery — look completely different.

The Hormonal Factor: Why Women's Energy Works in Cycles

Men's hormonal cycles operate on a 24-hour loop — they wake up with high testosterone levels (which fuel focus and motivation), and by night, their energy naturally drops before resetting the next day. This predictable pattern allows them to sustain a linear, high-drive work schedule without crashing as often.

Women, however, cycle through a 28-day hormonal rhythm, where energy levels, focus, and emotional resilience fluctuate throughout the month. Some weeks, they feel powerful, productive, and unstoppable. Other weeks, they feel introspective, sensitive, and in need of rest.

Burnout happens when women ignore these natural cycles and force themselves into a male-patterned work structure.

Instead of honoring their flow of energy, they try to be "on" all the time — leading to rapid depletion.

Men can push harder for longer.

Women need strategic rest and recalibration.

The solution? Women must stop treating their energy like an unlimited resource — and start managing it like a renewable one.

The Emotional Labor Overload

Burnout for women isn't just about workload — it's about the emotional labor they carry, often without realizing it.

Emotional labor is the unpaid, invisible work of managing emotions, relationships, and responsibilities.

Women, more than men, are expected to:

- Manage the emotions of those around them — partners, children, employees, clients.
- Maintain a household and social calendar (even while running businesses or careers).
- Act as the emotional anchor for friends and family.
- Absorb other people's stress while keeping their own emotions in check.

A woman might run a business all day, then come home and be expected to handle childcare, housework, and emotional support for her family.

A female CEO might carry the same leadership stress as her male counterparts, but also be expected to maintain warmth, emotional intelligence, and team morale — something male leaders are rarely questioned about.

The result? Women don't just burn out physically. They burn out emotionally.

Their nervous systems are constantly activated, never getting the full reset they need. This leads to chronic stress, anxiety, and exhaustion that no amount of time off can fix.

Men are allowed to focus on work. Women are expected to "do it all." And that's why their burnout is deeper, heavier, and harder to recover from.

The "Perfectionism Trap" and Why Women Feel They Must Work Harder

Men believe they are worthy because they exist. Women believe they must prove they are worthy.

One of the biggest reasons women burn out faster than men is because of perfectionism — the belief that they must:

- Get everything right.
- Never fail.
- Always be prepared before taking the next step.

Men are conditioned to try, fail, and keep moving — which allows them to take risks, make mistakes, and still progress forward without guilt.

Women, however, are conditioned to believe that if they aren't perfect, they aren't enough.

They over-prepare, waiting until they are 100% "ready" before launching something.

Fast-Track Millionairess

They over-deliver, adding more work than necessary just to justify their value.

They overextend themselves, believing that resting or slowing down means they are failing.

The result? Women work harder, longer, and burn out faster — while men take bigger risks, work fewer hours, and still succeed.

The solution? Women need to release perfectionism and start trusting that their value is not measured by how much they do — but by who they are.

The Signs of Burnout in Women (That Are Different from Men's)

Men and women experience burnout differently. While men often show burnout through anger, detachment, and disengagement, women's burnout is more internalized and emotional.

Burnout Signs in Women:

- **Chronic exhaustion** — Even after sleep, you still feel drained.
- **Brain fog and lack of clarity** — Struggling to make decisions, feeling mentally "fuzzy."
- **Resentment toward work or people** — Feeling unappreciated, undervalued, or irritated by things that didn't bother you before.
- **Disconnection from joy** — You stop feeling excited about things you once loved.
- **Guilt over resting** — Even when exhausted, you feel bad for slowing down.
- **Over-giving without receiving** — Feeling like you do everything for others but get little in return.
- **Feeling emotionally overwhelmed** — Crying easily, feeling overly sensitive, or struggling to regulate emotions.
- **Extreme fear** — Anxiety, panic, or deep worry about failing, disappointing others, or losing control.

If you recognize these signs, your body is trying to tell you something. And if you ignore it, burnout will only deepen — until your mind, body, and emotions force you to stop.

The Feminine Approach to Healing Burnout

Rest is not a reward. Rest is a strategy.

Because women's burnout is different, their recovery needs to be different too. It's not just about taking a vacation or "cutting back" — it's about rewiring their relationship with success, work, and self-worth so that burnout doesn't happen in the first place.

The New Model: Energy First, Productivity Second.

Women need to build businesses, careers, and lives that work with their energy — not against it. This means:

- **Honoring energy cycles.** Instead of working at the same pace every day, lean into your natural highs and lows. Schedule deep work during peak energy days and allow for rest or creative work when energy is lower.
- **Releasing the 'Do-It-All' Syndrome.** You don't have to be everything for everyone. Delegate, set boundaries, and let go of roles that drain you.
- **Building recovery into your schedule.** Rest isn't something you do after burnout — it's something you do to prevent burnout. Schedule breaks before you need them.
- **Letting go of perfectionism.** Done is better than perfect. You do not need to be 100% ready — you are already enough.
- **Learning to receive.** Success should not come from endless giving. Learn to allow support, financial abundance, and ease into your life.

The *Fast-Track Millionairess* Approach: Balancing Drive with Well-Being

Burnout is not a badge of honor. It is a warning sign that something needs to change.

- **You can be wildly successful** without exhaustion.
- **You can make life-changing money** without burnout.
- **You can be powerful and prosperous** while honoring your body, mind, and soul.
- **You can scale your wealth** without sacrificing your well-being.

Because true success isn't just about what you create — it's about how you *feel* while creating it.

How to Work with Your Natural Rhythms Instead of Against Them

Your energy is your greatest business asset — when you learn to work with it, instead of fighting against it.

Women are not designed to operate in linear, 24/7 productivity cycles like men. Yet, traditional success models expect them to show up the same way, every single day — regardless of energy levels, intuition, or emotional needs.

This is why so many women burn out.

Their bodies and minds crave flow, variation, and renewal, but they are forcing themselves into a structure that only rewards constant output.

The truth? Women's greatest power comes when they align their work, business, and life with their natural rhythms.

Here's how to do it.

Fast-Track Millionairess

Understand Your Energy Cycles (And Why They Matter)

Unlike men, whose hormones reset daily, women's energy fluctuates in cycles — both monthly and seasonally. These cycles influence focus, creativity, productivity, and emotional resilience.

When you stop expecting yourself to be "on" all the time and start working with these rhythms, you unlock a new level of ease, success, and well-being.

The Monthly Rhythm (The Four-Phase Energy Cycle)

If you are still cycling, your body naturally moves through four distinct energy phases each month. Even if you're not menstruating, your body still follows a similar rise and fall of energy — just like the moon, the tides, and the seasons.

Each phase impacts how you work best, what tasks feel easiest, and when you need rest.

Phase 1: The Rest and Reflect Phase (Menstrual / New Moon / Winter Energy)

- Best for: Deep reflection, journaling, reviewing business progress, intuitive decision-making.
- Work with it: Lower-intensity work, deep focus, planning, setting new intentions.
- Avoid: Forcing high-energy tasks or launching something new.

Phase 2: The Creative Power Phase (Follicular / Waxing Moon / Spring Energy)

- Best for: Brainstorming, creative projects, new ideas, setting things in motion.
- Work with it: Content creation, writing, strategizing, networking.
- Avoid: Overloading your schedule too early — build momentum gradually.

Phase 3: The Magnetic Action Phase (Ovulation / Full Moon / Summer Energy)

- Best for: High-energy tasks, public speaking, launches, marketing, visibility work.
- Work with it: Pitching offers, recording videos, hosting webinars, making bold moves.
- Avoid: Wasting this energy on small, low-impact tasks — this is your time to show up big.

Phase 4: The Slow Down and Review Phase (Luteal / Waning Moon / Autumn Energy)

- Best for: Editing, refining, completing unfinished work, organizing, deep self-care.
- Work with it: Systemizing your business, tying up loose ends, reducing unnecessary commitments.
- Avoid: Overloading your calendar — your body is calling for more internal focus.

Game-Changer: If you start structuring your workload to match these phases, you'll find yourself working less, creating more, and feeling far more balanced.

Plan Your Work Around Your Peak Productivity Windows

Not all hours are created equal — use your best ones wisely.

Most people structure their workday based on external demands (emails, meetings, deadlines) rather than their own peak energy times.

Women's energy naturally rises and falls throughout the day, and knowing your high-focus and low-focus hours allows you to get more done without burning yourself out.

Morning Peak (6 AM – 12 PM)

- Best for: Deep work, creative problem-solving, writing, focused projects.
- Work with it: Block out distraction-free time for your most important work.

Afternoon Dip (12 PM – 4 PM)

- Best for: Administrative tasks, meetings, emails, social media engagement.
- Work with it: Use this time for easier, lower-energy activities rather than deep focus work.

Evening Flow (4 PM – 9 PM)

- Best for: Learning, reflection, planning, visioning, inspiration-based work.
- Work with it: Journal, brainstorm new ideas, read, visualize the next level of success.

Stop expecting yourself to be productive all day long. Instead, align your most important tasks with when your energy is naturally strongest.

Balance Doing with Receiving (Feminine and Masculine Energy in Business)

Hustle is masculine. Flow is feminine. Success needs both.

Most women have been taught to push, force, and grind their way to success — relying only on masculine energy (action, strategy, logic, structure).

But feminine energy — the energy of receptivity, intuition, ease, and flow — is just as powerful.

The *Fast-Track Millionairess* approach is about learning to balance both.

Masculine Energy (Doing Mode): Setting goals, taking strategic action, structuring systems, financial planning.

Fast-Track Millionairess

Feminine Energy (Receiving Mode): Tuning into intuition, allowing ease, aligning decisions with energy cycles, working with flow instead of force.

When you balance the two, business becomes effortless. You work hard when it's time to push forward — but you also allow space for opportunities, creativity, and rest.

How to shift into a feminine energy business model:

- Start your day with intention, not obligation — check in with what feels aligned before jumping into tasks.
- Follow energy over schedule — if you feel inspired, create. If you feel exhausted, pause.
- Learn to trust that ease is productive — some of your biggest business breakthroughs will come when you're in flow, not forcing.

Work with Seasons, Not Just Days

Women are seasonal beings — meaning your business growth, creativity, and energy expand and contract just like nature.

Spring (Growth Mode): New ideas, launching offers, high-creation energy.

Summer (Expansion Mode): Visibility, public speaking, launching big projects.

Autumn (Refinement Mode): Organizing, tweaking, adjusting, reviewing business progress.

Winter (Rest Mode): Deep inner work, planning for the next level, preparing for rebirth.

The mistake most women make? Trying to be in 'Summer' mode all year long.

When you honor the seasons of growth and rest, you build a business that supports your long-term success.

Protect Your Energy Like You Protect Your Wealth

Your energy is your most valuable currency — spend it wisely.

Instead of working harder, focus on optimizing your energy flow with these key shifts:

- Start every work session with a 2-minute check-in — What's your energy level? What would feel best to work on now?
- Take micro-breaks — Move, breathe, stretch every 90 minutes to reset your focus.
- Say NO to energy-draining work, people, or obligations — The more you cut out, the more space you create for aligned success.
- Prioritize 'nothing time' — Moments of stillness allow your greatest ideas and clarity to surface.

Remember: The more energy you protect, the more wealth you can create — because burnout never built an empire.

The *Fast-Track Millionairess* Energy Equation: More Flow, Less Force

Success doesn't come from pushing harder — it comes from aligning smarter.

- You don't have to work the same way every day.
- You don't have to be productive all the time.
- You don't have to force success — it can come with ease.

Because when women stop fighting their natural rhythms?

They stop burning out — and start thriving.

Feminine Energy Vs. Masculine Energy in Business

Success isn't just about how hard you work — it's about how aligned you are with your energy.

Fast-Track Millionairess

For centuries, business and success have been defined through a masculine lens — one that prioritizes hustle, logic, and linear growth over intuition, flow, and sustainable expansion.

While masculine energy is essential for structure, decision-making, and execution, it is not the only way to create wealth — and for many women, relying solely on masculine energy leads to burnout rather than long-term success.

True success comes from balancing both masculine and feminine energies — using strategy and flow, action and intuition, drive and rest to build a business that thrives without depleting you.

Here's how to shift into a balanced success model that honors both.

What Is Masculine Energy in Business?

Masculine energy is the doing energy — it is action-driven, goal-oriented, and structured.

It thrives on logic, competition, and forward motion, making it powerful for:

- Setting clear goals and strategies
- Taking decisive action and making fast decisions
- Building scalable systems and business structures
- Pushing forward despite obstacles
- Leading with confidence and authority

Masculine energy is what gets things done — it moves a business forward, creates financial systems, and ensures stability and growth.

The Strength of Masculine Energy: It helps you stay focused, determined, and disciplined.

The Danger of Overusing It: It can lead to burnout, rigidity, and disconnection from intuition.

Fast-Track Millionairess

When women rely too much on their masculine energy, they push harder than necessary, ignore their natural rhythms, and feel exhausted from constantly "doing" without allowing themselves to receive.

What Is Feminine Energy in Business?

Feminine energy is the being energy — it is intuitive, receptive, creative, and fluid.

It thrives on alignment, ease, and deep connection, making it powerful for:

- Tuning into intuition and making soul-aligned decisions
- Attracting opportunities instead of chasing them
- Creating magnetic offers that resonate deeply with others
- Embracing rest, reflection, and sustainable success
- Building relationships based on trust, authenticity, and connection

Feminine energy allows you to create from inspiration, trust your inner knowing, and allow business to unfold with flow rather than force.

The Strength of Feminine Energy: It helps you build a business that feels aligned, joyful, and magnetic.

The Danger of Overusing It: It can lead to lack of structure, indecision, and passivity if not balanced with action.

When women lean too far into feminine energy without balancing it with inner masculine energy structure, they can struggle to take action, price confidently, or scale their business effectively.

The Biggest Energy Imbalance Women Face in Business

Most women default to one extreme or the other:

Too much masculine energy → Burnout

Fast-Track Millionairess

You're constantly pushing, forcing, and grinding, leaving you exhausted and disconnected from your intuition.

Too much feminine energy → Stagnation

You have big dreams and creativity, but you lack the structure, pricing confidence, or action to make them happen.

The *Fast-Track Millionairess* approach is about balancing both — so you can create massive success without burnout or hesitation.

How to Balance Feminine and Masculine Energy in Business

The goal isn't to choose one energy over the other — it's to learn when to use each one for maximum impact.

Here's how to integrate both into your daily business strategy:

Masculine Energy (Doing)

Set clear financial goals — Know exactly how much you want to earn and create a strategy to get there.

Take decisive action — Make decisions quickly and trust yourself instead of overthinking.

Use systems and automation — Create workflows that save time and scale your success.

Be consistent — Masculine energy thrives in discipline and structure. Set a schedule and stick to it.

Track success metrics — Monitor business growth, client conversions, and financial progress with logic, not just intuition.

Masculine energy is what turns your ideas into reality.

Fast-Track Millionairess

Feminine Energy (Being)

Follow intuitive nudges — If something feels aligned, trust it. If something feels off, don't force it.

Create from inspiration, not pressure — Work on projects that light you up instead of hustling for the sake of it.

Use attraction over chase — Instead of constantly "selling," allow your energy to magnetize opportunities to you.

Honor your energy cycles — Work with your natural flow rather than forcing productivity when you're depleted.

Rest and recharge without guilt — Success is not about constantly doing — it's also about allowing.

Feminine energy is what makes your business feel fulfilling, creative, and sustainable.

How to Apply This in Real Life

Sales and Marketing

Masculine Approach: Direct sales, structured campaigns, tracking conversions.
Feminine Approach: Storytelling, brand magnetism, relationship-based marketing.

Money and Pricing

Masculine Approach: Set clear financial goals, price confidently, track income.
Feminine Approach: Align your pricing with your energy, feel into what *feels* right.

Work Schedule

Masculine Approach: Structured work hours, action-based productivity.
Feminine Approach: Flexible time for creativity, honoring energy cycles.

Scaling Your Business

- Masculine Approach: Systems, automation, hiring, delegation.
- Feminine Approach: Soul-aligned expansion, intuitive business growth.

The Key to Success: Use masculine energy to create structure — but let feminine energy lead the way.

The *Fast-Track Millionairess* Success Formula

Masculine Energy → Gets you to the goal.

Feminine Energy → Ensures the journey feels good.

- You don't have to hustle like a man to succeed.
- You don't have to sit back and wait for success to come to you.
- You get to create wealth in a way that feels aligned, powerful, and natural to you.

Because when you balance masculine strategy with feminine flow?

You don't just create success — you create ease, joy, and freedom along the way.

How to Create Sustainable Momentum Without Depletion

Success isn't just about moving fast — it's about moving in a way that you can sustain long-term.

Many women believe they must push harder, do more, and keep up a relentless pace to be successful. They fear that if they slow down, they'll lose momentum, opportunities, or income.

But momentum isn't about speed — it's about consistency.

If success comes at the cost of your health, happiness, or sanity, it's not success — it's self-sacrifice.

Fast-Track Millionairess

The *Fast-Track Millionairess* approach is about creating momentum that is sustainable, energizing, and aligned — so that you don't just reach success, but you can actually enjoy it once you get there.

Here's how to do it.

Stop Using Willpower — Start Using Systems

Willpower is unreliable. Systems create consistency without the burnout.

If you are relying on motivation or pushing through exhaustion to keep momentum, you are setting yourself up for burnout.

Instead, create systems that carry you forward — even when your energy is low.

- Batch work and automate — Instead of working in constant output mode, batch-create content, schedule tasks in advance, and automate repetitive work.
- Use templates and repeatable processes — Every time you do something more than once, systemize it.
- Have a business model that works even when you rest — Offer digital products, courses, or recurring income streams that keep generating income without constant effort.

Momentum is not about working harder — it's about making success easier to maintain.

Work in Sprints, Not Marathons

Women's energy is cyclical — not linear. If you try to work at the same intensity every day, you will burn out.

Instead of working at a constant, unsustainable pace, embrace energy sprints — focused, high-impact work sessions followed by intentional recovery.

Fast-Track Millionairess

High-energy days: Focus on big, deep work (strategy, launches, sales, creation).

Low-energy days: Focus on maintenance work (admin, reflection, self-care, creative play).

Momentum doesn't mean working non-stop — it means knowing when to accelerate and when to pause.

Honor the Power of 'Aligned Action' Over Forced Action

Not all action leads to results — only aligned action does.

Many women waste energy on busyness instead of true momentum — doing things because they feel like they "should" rather than because they are truly necessary.

Before taking action, ask: Is this necessary? Is this aligned? Is this moving me forward in the simplest way possible?

Prioritize needle-moving activities — Instead of doing 100 things, focus on the 3 things that actually create results.

Let go of tasks that drain you — If something feels heavy, frustrating, or pointless, either delegate it or drop it.

Momentum is not about doing everything — it's about doing the right things with the right energy.

Learn to Build 'Success Stamina'

Most people can go fast for a short period. Few can sustain success for the long haul.

True momentum is about building stamina — the ability to keep moving without depleting yourself.

Pace yourself — Don't go all-in at 100% and burn out. Sustainable success is built step by step, not in one massive push.

Protect your recovery time — Take breaks before you need them. When you schedule rest, you don't have to recover from burnout.

Follow the 80/20 rule — 80% of results come from 20% of actions. Focus on the most powerful activities and eliminate unnecessary work.

Success isn't about working the hardest — it's about knowing how to maintain your energy for the long run.

Detach from the 'Overachiever' Identity

Being busy is not the same as being successful.

Many women fall into the overachiever trap, believing that:

- The more they work, the more valuable they are.
- If they stop hustling, everything will fall apart.
- Resting means they aren't "doing enough."

The truth? Success comes faster when you stop overworking and start working with intention.

Ask yourself: What if it was easy?

Challenge the belief that success must be 'earned' through struggle. Reframe rest as a success strategy — not a weakness.

The wealthiest women aren't the ones working the hardest. They are the ones who have mastered the art of working smarter.

Create a Momentum Loop That Fuels You

Your energy, emotions, and actions are all connected — momentum comes from keeping them in alignment.

Here's how to create a momentum loop that is self-sustaining, not draining:

Step 1: Fuel Your Energy — Start each day with practices that energize you (meditation, movement, morning journaling).

Step 2: Align Your Actions — Work on what feels right, not just what feels urgent.

Step 3: Acknowledge Small Wins — Momentum builds when you recognize progress instead of just chasing the next goal.

Step 4: Celebrate and Integrate — After hitting milestones, take time to rest, recalibrate, and allow success to land.

Step 5: Repeat with Ease — When energy is feeling like it is restored, repeat the loop — without force.

Momentum doesn't come from hustling — it comes from staying in energetic alignment.

Know When to Pause (Without Fear of Losing Progress)

Pausing is not the same as stopping. Sometimes, stepping back is the fastest way forward.

One of the biggest fears women have is that if they slow down, they will lose progress.

This is false.

Momentum is not just about speed — it's about direction. Taking intentional pauses allows you to:

- Reassess whether your actions are aligned.
- Replenish your creative and physical energy.
- Avoid making decisions from exhaustion instead of clarity.

The most successful women are not the ones who never stop — they are the ones who know when to pause, reflect, and come back stronger.

The *Fast-Track Millionairess* Momentum Formula

- **Sustainable success is not about grinding harder** — it's about creating systems, rhythms, and aligned action.
- **Momentum comes from working with your energy** — not against it.
- **You don't have to run at full speed** all the time to stay successful.
- **When you stop chasing, forcing, and overworking** — success flows to you with ease.

Because the best kind of momentum?

The kind that lasts.

Chapter 4: Jealousy and Competition — Turning Triggers into Power

How Emotional Jealousy Can Hold Women Back Rather Than Propel Them Forward

Comparison kills joy. Jealousy destroys friendships. Judgment defines the judge — not the one being judged.

Women are often taught that other women are their competition. From a young age, they are conditioned to compare, compete, and, in many cases, tear each other down instead of lifting each other up.

But here's the hard truth:

Women are far nastier about each other than men are about each other — and this has to stop.

For feminine energy to come into balance in the world, women must release jealousy, comparison, and judgment and step into empowered collaboration, support, and collective success.

Because a woman in her power does not compete. She creates.

The Destructive Cycle of Jealousy and Comparison

Jealousy is not just an emotion — it is an energy drain. It pulls women out of their own power and keeps them trapped in cycles of insecurity, self-doubt, and resentment.

And yet, it happens everywhere:

- The woman who gossips about a successful friend rather than celebrating her.

- The entrepreneur who resents another woman's business growth instead of learning from it.
- The colleague who silently judges another woman's confidence, thinking, *Who does she think she is?*

When women waste energy tearing each other down, they rob themselves of their own success.

Instead of using jealousy as a trigger for growth and inspiration, many women allow it to hold them back, destroy friendships, and block abundance.

Comparison is the fastest way to lose joy. The moment a woman stops focusing on her own path and starts obsessing over what someone else has, she disconnects from her own potential.

Why Do Women Judge Each Other So Harshly?

Judging anyone does not define the person being judged — it defines the person who feels the need to judge.

Women have been conditioned to see each other as threats rather than allies. Unlike men, who often form competitive but still supportive networks, women are more likely to:

- Tear down other women's success instead of learning from it.
- Judge each other's choices — career paths, parenting styles, relationships, and appearances.
- Blame men for their struggles instead of owning their power to change their circumstances.
- Feel threatened by another woman's success — as if someone else's achievements mean there is less available for them.
- Use emotional tactics to tear each other down — subtle jabs, passive-aggressive comments, or exclusion from groups.

This needs to stop.

This conditioning runs deep, and it's rooted in generations of scarcity thinking — the belief that only a few women can rise, so others must be pushed down. Women must also recognize that their biggest obstacle is not men — it is their own limiting beliefs about themselves.

The truth:

- No man can take away your power unless you allow it.
- No man can stop you from creating wealth, success, and freedom.
- Blaming men or historic treatment of women is a distraction — taking ownership is the real work.
- Another woman's success takes nothing away from you.
- Her beauty, her wealth, her confidence — none of it diminishes your own.
- There is no limit to success. When one woman wins, she shows the path for others to win, too.

When women stop blaming and start creating, they become unstoppable.

The Hidden Cost of Jealousy and Competition

Many women believe jealousy will motivate them to do better — but in reality, it does the opposite.

Here's what happens when jealousy is left unchecked:

It Distracts from Your Own Path

The more time you spend watching someone else's success, the less time you spend creating your own.

It Blocks Opportunities

A jealous mind is a closed mind. Women who judge or resent others often repel the very opportunities they desire.

Fast-Track Millionairess

It Damages Friendships and Relationships

Comparison kills joy, and Jealousy destroys trust and connection. Many friendships fall apart simply because one woman cannot celebrate another woman's success.

It Lowers Your Frequency and Repels Abundance

Jealousy is rooted in scarcity thinking — the belief that success is limited. But wealth, joy, and success expand for those who believe there is enough for everyone.

It Makes Success Feel Empty

Women who climb to success by competing, tearing others down, or holding resentment often find that when they arrive... they feel unfulfilled.

It Creates a Victim Mindset

Blaming men, society, history, or external circumstances for lack of success is the fastest way to stay stuck. Women must shift from complaining about the system to learning how to win within it.

It Reinforces Disempowerment

As long as women see men as the reason for their struggles, they are giving away their power. The moment they realize that success is entirely within their control, everything changes.

It's Exhausting

Jealousy keeps women stuck in a negative thinking cycle that diminishes their power, and directly blocks the flow of their naturally buoyant and creative life-force.

Success is not just about achieving more — it's about how you feel while achieving it.

Fast-Track Millionairess

Turning Jealousy into Power

Jealousy is not a sign that you are failing — it is a sign that you are seeing a possibility for yourself.

Instead of allowing jealousy to steal your energy, block your opportunities, and destroy relationships, use it as a guide.

Recognize the Trigger

When you feel jealous, pause and ask: What is this emotion telling me?

Reframe It as a Lesson

Instead of thinking, *Why do they have that and I don't?* shift to: *What is this person showing me about what is possible for me?*

Shift from Comparison to Inspiration

Instead of resenting another's success, use it as proof that you can have it too.

Celebrate Her Success (Yes, Really!)

The fastest way to shift jealousy? Celebrate the very thing that triggered you:

- Send her a message congratulating her.
- Speak positively about her success to others.
- Let yourself feel joy for her — because joy attracts more success into your own life.

Take Full Ownership of Your Life

Instead of blaming men, the system, or the past, ask yourself:

- What can I do today to move forward in my own success?
- Where have I been playing small, and how can I step into my full power?

- Am I willing to take radical responsibility for my own life?

Take Action Toward Your Own Goals

Instead of staying stuck in watching mode, shift into creating mode. Ask yourself: What is one step I can take today toward my own dreams?

The secret? When women fully own their success, they stop needing to judge or compete — because they are too busy creating their own abundance.

Ending the Cycle: Women Lifting Women

The future of feminine power depends on women uplifting — not competing with — each other.

For too long, women have been conditioned to tear each other down instead of build each other up. But that time is over.

- Women do not need to dim their light to make others comfortable.
- There is more than enough success, wealth, love, and happiness for everyone.
- When women rise together, they rewrite the rules of power.

Your success is inevitable when you learn to celebrate — not resent — the success of others.

Because the truth is simple:

A rising woman lifts others with her. Always.

Reframing Jealousy as Inspiration Instead of Self-Sabotage

Jealousy is often treated as a negative emotion, something to be ashamed of or suppressed. But in reality, jealousy is not the problem — the way we respond to it is.

Fast-Track Millionairess

Most women are never taught how to process jealousy in a healthy way. They either ignore it, letting it build into resentment, or allow it to spiral into self-doubt and insecurity. But jealousy is actually one of the most valuable signals you can receive — a signpost revealing what you deeply desire for yourself.

The question is not *How do I get rid of jealousy?* but rather *How do I use it to my advantage?*

When you learn to see jealousy as inspiration instead of a reason to self-sabotage, it becomes a powerful tool for personal and financial growth.

How Jealousy Turns into Self-Sabotage

For many women, jealousy triggers a downward spiral of destructive behaviors that keep them stuck. It doesn't just steal joy; it actively blocks success, relationships, and self-worth.

When jealousy is unchecked, it often leads to:

Comparison and Self-Doubt

Instead of seeing someone else's success as proof of possibility, many women see it as proof that they are behind, not good enough, or incapable of achieving the same.

Instead of feeling inspired, they shrink, telling themselves, *That could never be me.*

Resentment Toward Other Women

Jealousy, when left unchecked, turns into bitterness. Instead of admiring another woman's achievements, some women start searching for reasons to discredit her success — telling themselves, *She had an advantage* or *She's not that great anyway.*

This mindset creates division among women, blocking connection, collaboration, and mutual growth.

Inaction and Avoidance

Some women become paralyzed by jealousy. Instead of letting it push them to take action, they avoid pursuing their goals, believing the gap between where they are and where they want to be is too big to close.

Gossip and Quiet Sabotage

When jealousy festers, it often leads to tearing others down — whether through criticism, passive-aggressive comments, or outright exclusion. Instead of confronting their own feelings, some women try to diminish others to make themselves feel better.

A Scarcity Mindset That Repels Success

At its core, jealousy thrives on scarcity thinking — the false belief that there is not enough success, money, or happiness to go around.

This leads to fear-based thinking, where women subconsciously block their own success because they are too focused on what others have instead of creating their own path.

Unchecked jealousy does not just harm friendships and professional relationships — it prevents women from stepping into their full power. Energy spent on comparison, judgment, and resentment is energy that could have been used for growth, expansion, and success.

The Truth About Jealousy: It's a Signpost, Not a Curse

Jealousy is not a sign that you are failing. It is a sign that you are seeing a possibility for yourself.

When you feel jealous of another woman's success, beauty, confidence, or wealth, it does not mean she has something you can never have. It means that on some level, you know you are capable of achieving the same.

The women who trigger you the most? They are often mirrors of your own untapped potential.

When you start seeing jealousy as a guide instead of a threat, everything shifts. Instead of feeling insecure or resentful, you can start asking:

- What does this jealousy reveal about my own desires?
- What about her success is triggering me — and why?
- Am I allowing myself to pursue what I really want, or have I been holding back?

This mindset shift is not about ignoring your feelings — it is about using them as fuel for growth instead of self-destruction.

How to Turn Jealousy into Power and Success

Jealousy holds most women back because they see it as something negative instead of an opportunity for expansion. The key is to reframe it into a source of motivation and inspiration.

Recognize Jealousy as A Sign of Clarity

Instead of reacting emotionally, pause and ask: *What is this feeling revealing about what I truly want?*

If you feel jealous of someone's financial success, career, relationships, or confidence, it is because part of you knows you are capable of having the same.

Reframe It as Proof of Possibility

Jealousy often means you are witnessing someone doing something you didn't believe was possible for yourself.

Instead of thinking, *Why her and not me?*, shift to *If she can do it, so can I.*

Fast-Track Millionairess

Instead of seeing her success as proof of your lack, see it as evidence that the life you desire is achievable.

Turn Jealousy into Research

Instead of resenting someone's success, study how they achieved it. Ask:

- What actions did she take?
- What mindset shifts did she embrace?
- What risks did she take that I have been avoiding?

Use this as a learning opportunity rather than an excuse to stay stuck.

Channel the Energy into Action

Jealousy is an intense emotion. If you sit in it too long, it becomes destructive. Instead, use it as fuel to take meaningful steps toward your own goals.

Make a plan. Set a deadline. Take one bold action today.

Celebrate Others to Attract More Success into Your Own Life

One of the fastest ways to dissolve jealousy is to genuinely celebrate the success of those who trigger it.

Instead of secretly resenting someone, try this:

- Congratulate them.
- Share their work or success with others.
- Speak positively about them — even when they aren't around.

The more you celebrate success in others, the more you attract it into your own life.

Fast-Track Millionairess

Shifting from Scarcity to Abundance

At the core of jealousy is the false belief that success is limited — that if one woman achieves something, there is *less* available for others. This scarcity mindset is one of the biggest blocks to wealth, happiness, and personal growth.

- Success is not a finite resource. There is room for every woman to thrive.
- Another woman's success does not take anything away from you. It simply shows what is possible.
- Women do not need to compete — they need to collaborate.

Jealousy only holds power over you if you let it. But the moment you reframe it as inspiration instead of self-sabotage, it stops being an obstacle and starts becoming a pathway to your highest potential.

The *Fast-Track Millionairess* Jealousy Reframe Formula

- **Jealousy is not a sign of failure — it is a sign of desire.** What triggers you most is often pointing you toward your own untapped potential.
- **Another woman's success does not take anything away from you.** There is no shortage of wealth, happiness, or achievement — only a shortage of belief.
- **Comparison steals your joy, but inspiration fuels your success.** Shift from "Why her?" to "If she can do it, so can I."
- **Celebrating others accelerates your own growth.** When you support women instead of resenting them, you open yourself to more abundance.
- **Women do not need to compete — they need to collaborate.** True feminine power is built through connection, not division.

When you stop judging, comparing, and resenting — and start learning, celebrating, and taking action — you move from jealousy to empowerment, from scarcity to abundance, and from competition to limitless success.

The Power of Collaboration Over Competition

For centuries, women have been taught to compete with one another instead of rising together. Whether in business, relationships, or social circles, the unspoken rule has been that another woman's success somehow threatens your own.

But this is an illusion.

The most powerful, wealthy, and fulfilled women understand one thing: Collaboration is far more powerful than competition.

Competition among women is a relic of an outdated system — one that told women there was only room for a few at the top. But in reality, success is limitless, and when women stop competing and start collaborating, they create more wealth, more power, and more impact than they ever could alone.

Why Women Are Conditioned to Compete

Women have been subtly (and not so subtly) trained to see each other as threats rather than allies. This conditioning runs deep and shows up in ways many women don't even recognize.

Scarcity Mindset

Women have historically been given fewer opportunities in business, leadership, and wealth-building. This has led to the belief that there is not enough success to go around.

Instead of seeing the world as abundant, many women operate from a mindset of lack, believing that if one woman wins, another must lose.

Comparison Culture

From a young age, women are encouraged to compare themselves — to each other's looks, relationships, achievements, and status.

This constant measuring-up creates jealousy, insecurity, and the belief that another woman's success is a reflection of one's own inadequacy.

Divide and Conquer Tactics

Society has long benefited from women being divided. When women are busy tearing each other down, they are too distracted to challenge the systems that limit them.

Instead of forming strong, wealth-building, power-creating alliances, women are often pitted against each other in ways that prevent them from collective success.

But Here's the Truth

- The world does not run out of money when another woman becomes wealthy.
- Another woman's beauty does not make you less beautiful.
- Another woman's success does not make you less capable of achieving your own.

Women have spent far too long wasting energy on competition when they could be using that energy to create something greater together.

How Collaboration Creates More Success for Women

When women collaborate, they tap into exponential power. They create networks of shared resources, knowledge, and opportunities that accelerate success for everyone involved.

Here's why collaboration always wins:

It Multiplies Opportunities Instead of Limiting Them

When women support each other, they open doors instead of closing them.

Fast-Track Millionairess

A woman in your network could introduce you to your next business partner, investor, or opportunity that changes your life.

It Expands Financial Success for All Involved

Collaboration in business allows women to leverage each other's skills, audiences, and resources instead of trying to do everything alone.

Partnerships, joint ventures, and shared audiences create bigger impact, more income, and faster growth.

It Builds Long-Term Power Instead of Short-Term Wins

Competition is a temporary mindset — it keeps you in survival mode.

Collaboration is a legacy mindset — it builds long-term influence, wealth, and networks that continue growing over time.

It Shifts Women from Scarcity Thinking to Abundance Thinking

The moment you see another woman's success as proof of possibility instead of a personal threat, you shift into a mindset of limitless opportunity.

It Creates A Ripple Effect of Empowerment

When one woman rises and brings others with her, she changes the game for every woman who comes after her.

The most successful women are not the ones who competed their way to the top — they are the ones who built a network of powerful allies who rose together.

How to Shift from Competition to Collaboration

If you've been conditioned to compete, it can take conscious effort to rewire your mindset toward collaboration.

Fast-Track Millionairess

Here's how to start.

Stop Seeing Other Women as Rivals

Instead of thinking, *How do I beat her?* Shift to *How can we grow together?*

Look for ways to support, amplify, and work with other women instead of against them.

Share Knowledge and Opportunities

Women often hoard information because they fear others will "take" their success. But success expands when it is shared.

If you know of an opportunity, pass it on. If you can connect two women who could help each other, do it.

Celebrate and Promote Other Women's Success

Instead of feeling triggered by someone's achievements, celebrate them.

Speak positively about women behind their backs. Promote their work. Lift them up.

Build Strong Female Networks

Surround yourself with women who are also committed to collaboration.

The stronger your circle, the faster your success.

Be the Woman Who Proves That Collaboration Is the Future

Instead of waiting for the world to change, be the woman who leads the shift.

Show that women working together create more power, wealth, and influence than women working alone.

Fast-Track Millionairess

The most powerful woman in the room is not the one who competes. It's the one who lifts others up while rising.

The *Fast-Track Millionairess* Collaboration Formula

- **Competition is outdated.** Collaboration is the new model of power.
- **Another person's success is not a threat** — it is an invitation for you to rise, too.
- **The fastest way to accelerate your success** is to create powerful female alliances.
- **Women thrive when they support each other**, not when they tear each other down.
- **The world changes when women rise together** instead of trying to outrun each other or trying to outrun men.

When you stop competing, comparing, and working alone — and start connecting, collaborating, and rising together — you step into a new level of success, wealth, and empowerment that is limitless.

Building A Mindset of Abundance Instead of Scarcity

For too long, women have been conditioned to believe that success, wealth, and opportunity are limited resources — that only a select few can have them. This scarcity mindset keeps women playing small, fearing competition, and holding themselves back from the wealth and freedom they desire.

But the truth is simple: *There is no limit to success.*

Money is not finite. Success is not capped. Opportunity is not a door that only opens for a chosen few. It is available to anyone who chooses to step into it.

The women who thrive — who create wealth, build businesses, and enjoy financial freedom — are not the ones who fight for scraps. They are the ones who rewrite the story, step into abundance, and refuse to believe in limitations.

The Scarcity Mindset: How It Holds Women Back

A scarcity mindset convinces women that success is a competition — that if someone else wins, they lose. It creates fear, insecurity, and resistance to growth.

Women stuck in scarcity thinking often:

Undercharge and Undervalue Their Work

They fear that if they price too high, no one will pay.

Instead of owning their worth, they discount their value.

Avoid Investing in Themselves

They hesitate to spend money on courses, coaching, or business growth, believing they "can't afford it."

They don't realize that investing in themselves is the fastest way to increase their earning power.

Hold Back from Taking Bold Opportunities

They fear failure more than they desire success.

They wait for "perfect timing" instead of taking action.

See Other Women as Competition Rather Than Allies

They believe there are only so many spots for success, so they resist collaboration.

They compare themselves to others instead of focusing on their own growth.

Stay Stuck in A Cycle of "Not Enough" Thinking

They believe there's not enough money, time, success, or opportunity.

They feel like they are always behind, instead of realizing they are in full control of their progress.

Scarcity Thinking Is the Fastest Way to Block Success

It keeps women playing small, staying in fear, and working far harder than necessary to achieve results.

But once a woman reframes her mindset from scarcity to abundance, everything changes.

Shifting into an Abundance Mindset

An abundance mindset does not mean ignoring reality. It means choosing to believe that growth, wealth, and opportunity are unlimited — and that you are fully capable of receiving them.

Here's how to shift into abundance thinking:

Recognize Where Scarcity Shows Up in Your Life

Scarcity thinking is sneaky. It often hides behind phrases like:

- "There's not enough money."
- "If she succeeds, I won't."
- "I have to work harder than everyone else to succeed."
- "If I charge too much, people won't pay."

When these thoughts come up, pause and ask: *Is this actually true, or is this just a belief I've been conditioned to accept?*

Most scarcity thoughts are not facts — they are inherited beliefs. And beliefs can be changed.

Fast-Track Millionairess

Shift from "Not Enough" to "More Than Enough"

Instead of focusing on lack, start training your brain to recognize abundance in every area of your life.

Money is always circulating, moving, and expanding. It is not running out.

Opportunities exist everywhere — you just have to be open to seeing them.

You are not in competition with anyone because there is more than enough success to go around.

The shift is simple but powerful:

- Instead of saying, *I can't afford this*, ask, *How can I create the money for this?*
- Instead of thinking, *That opportunity is out of my reach*, say, *I am fully capable of stepping into that level of success.*
- Instead of resenting someone else's wealth, use it as proof that it is possible for you, too.

Abundance is not about waiting for money or success to magically appear — it is about believing in possibilities and taking action accordingly.

Stop Hoarding and Start Circulating Wealth

Scarcity teaches women to hoard money, time, and resources out of fear — but hoarding creates stagnation. Wealth does not grow when it is held tightly.

Money is meant to move.

- When you invest in yourself, you expand your ability to earn more.
- When you pay for services, you create opportunities for others to thrive.
- When you give generously, you receive abundantly.

Fast-Track Millionairess

The women who build lasting wealth are not the ones who fear spending — it is the ones who circulate money with confidence, knowing it will return to them multiplied.

Instead of thinking, *If I spend this, I'll have less,* shift to:

- *Every dollar I spend on my growth comes back to me tenfold.*
- *Money flows to me effortlessly because I trust in abundance.*
- *I invest in myself because I am my greatest asset.*

Create Instead of Compete

A scarcity mindset forces women to compete for limited resources — but an abundance mindset empowers them to create their own opportunities.

You don't need to fight for a seat at someone else's table — you can build your own.

You don't need to chase clients — you can become magnetic to them.

You don't need to wait for someone to recognize your worth — you can step into it unapologetically.

Scarcity says, *There's not enough room for me.*
Abundance says, *I will create my own space.*

Scarcity says, *I have to prove myself before I can charge more.*
Abundance says, *I already bring immense value, and I will be paid accordingly.*

Scarcity says, *If she wins, I lose.*
Abundance says, *When she wins, she shows me what's possible.*

The women who step into abundance thinking build legacies, not just businesses.

Fast-Track Millionairess

Surround Yourself with Abundance Thinkers

Your mindset is shaped by the people you surround yourself with. If you spend time with people who complain about money, fear success, and believe in limitations, it will be harder to break free from scarcity thinking.

Instead, create a circle of abundance-minded women who:

- Celebrate success instead of resenting it
- Encourage bold moves instead of playing safe
- Invest in themselves without hesitation
- Believe in wealth as a tool for impact, freedom, and expansion

Your environment matters. If you want to shift into abundance, start immersing yourself in conversations, books, and mentors that reinforce limitless success.

The *Fast-Track Millionairess* Abundance Formula

- **Success is limitless.** The more women rise, the more space is created for others to rise, too.
- **Money is a renewable resource.** The more you circulate, invest, and expand, the more wealth flows to you.
- **There is no competition in abundance.** You don't need to fight for success — you need to align with it.
- **Your mindset shapes your reality.** When you expect growth, expansion, and wealth, you receive them.
- **When you trust in abundance, success flows effortlessly.**

Women who shift from scarcity to abundance thinking do not just make more money — they change the way they experience the world.

The moment you decide that there is more than enough for you, you will begin receiving more than you ever imagined.

PART TWO: FAST-TRACK WEALTH STRATEGIES

Practical Steps for Financial Independence and Business Success

Chapter 5: The Millionairess Blueprint — How to Build Wealth on Your Terms

You Must First Understand What Money Really Is

Most people spend their entire lives chasing money without ever truly understanding what it is, how it works, and why some people attract it effortlessly while others struggle with it endlessly.

Money is not what we have been led to believe. It is not power. It is not security. It is not even wealth.

At its core, money is a human invention — an unlimited resource designed to cover the timing difference between the exchange of value.

It is not real in the way that land, energy, or life force are real. It is a tool, a system of exchange, and — most importantly — it is created by human ambition, creativity, and value generation.

Money Is Not Limited — It Expands When Value Is Created

Many people believe that money is finite, that there is only so much of it to go around. But this is not true.

Money is printed when value is added to the system. Every time new businesses are created, new ideas are brought to life, or new products and services enter the market, banks and governments must print more money to match that growth.

The more people create, the more money circulates. This is why economies expand — because human creativity fuels innovation, which fuels demand, which requires more money to be put into circulation.

If you add value to the world, you increase the wealth of the entire system. Money is not something you "take" from others — it is something that grows when you participate in the system in a meaningful way.

Money is an effect, not a cause. It is a response to creation, not the source of it.

If you want more money, the question is not, How do I get more? The question is, How do I create more value?

Creativity, Not Intelligence, Is the Key to Wealth

One of the biggest myths about money is that intelligence determines financial success. People believe that the smartest, most educated, or most logical people will naturally be the wealthiest.

But in reality, creativity is the key factor in financial success.

Intelligence helps, but it is not the deciding factor. Many highly intelligent people struggle financially, while many creative risk-takers build empires.

Creativity leads to new solutions, innovations, and opportunities. It allows people to see beyond limitations, to create businesses, products, and services that did not exist before.

Money flows to those who bring something new into the world. Whether it is art, technology, ideas, or movements — creativity generates value, and value attracts wealth.

If you want to build wealth, start by building creativity.

Instead of asking, How can I make more money?, ask:

- What can I create that the world needs?
- How can I solve a problem in a way that others aren't?
- What unique gifts do I have that I am not using yet?

Fast-Track Millionairess

When you approach money with creativity, you open the door to unlimited financial potential.

Your Life Force Is the True Currency

Money is not the most valuable resource you have. Your life force — your time, energy, and attention — is.

Every single day, you exchange heartbeats for something.

- If you spend them creating, building, and adding value to the world, you get positive returns.
- If you waste them on gossip, drama, complaining, or spreading negativity, you get very little in return — or worse, negative returns.

The way you use your time and energy determines what you receive back from the system.

Wealth is not built by working harder — it is built by working in alignment with creation and value generation.

People who spend their life force wisely — by investing in their skills, creating solutions, and building meaningful connections — attract wealth naturally.

People who waste their life force — by focusing on what they lack, tearing others down, or staying trapped in negativity — struggle financially, because they are not adding value to the system.

Every action you take is an investment of energy. The question is:

- Are you investing your energy into growth, wealth, and expansion?
- Or are you spending it on fear, lack, and limitation?

The people who build wealth understand that money is just a reflection of where they invest their energy.

The *Fast-Track Millionairess* Money Formula

- **Money is a tool, not a goal.** It exists to facilitate the exchange of value, not to be chased endlessly.
- **Creativity, not intelligence, is the true key to wealth.** The most financially successful people are not necessarily the smartest — they are the most innovative.
- **Your life force is your greatest currency.** What you focus on, create, and contribute determines what you receive in return.
- **Positive energy creates positive financial returns.** If you use your heartbeats to create, solve, and inspire, money flows effortlessly to you.
- **There is no limit to money — only a limit to how much you create.** When you add value, the system expands, and more money is put into circulation.

If you want more money, stop chasing it. Start creating value, investing your energy wisely, and aligning yourself with expansion.

Because the women who build real wealth are not the ones who chase money.

They are the ones who understand it, create with it, and use it as a tool to build something bigger than themselves.

The *Fast-Track Millionairess* Model for Wealth Creation

For generations, wealth creation has been tied to trading time for money, climbing corporate ladders, and staying within predefined structures of success. Women have been taught that financial independence comes from working harder, following the rules, and waiting for permission to step into their power.

But the *Fast-Track Millionairess* model rejects all of that.

Fast-Track Millionairess

This is not about staying stuck in the rat race, working endlessly for someone else, or accepting limitations placed on your potential. This is about taking full ownership of your gifts, building wealth on your terms, and creating a life that aligns with your passions, talents, and purpose.

Wealth is not something you earn through suffering. It is something you create through alignment, strategy, and value.

Breaking Free from the Rat Race: Taking Ownership of Your Potential

Most people remain financially stuck because they have been conditioned to believe that success comes from:

- Working a fixed number of hours for a fixed amount of pay
- Following the "traditional" career path
- Playing it safe and avoiding risk
- Waiting for external validation or opportunities

But the truth is, you cannot build real wealth by following someone else's script.

To step into financial freedom, you must:

- Take full ownership of your potential — stop waiting for permission to create wealth and start designing it yourself.
- Detach from outdated success models — wealth is not about how many hours you work but about the value you create.
- Stop seeking external validation — no one else gets to define your worth, your business, or your impact.
- Decide that your financial success is inevitable — when you truly commit to the belief that wealth is available to you, you will take the actions necessary to create it.

The moment you decide to take full responsibility for your wealth, you move from being controlled by money to being the creator of it.

Fast-Track Millionairess

Building a Business That Aligns with You

The *Fast-Track Millionairess* model is not about fitting into someone else's system — it is about building wealth in a way that aligns with:

- Your passions — because financial success is easier when you genuinely enjoy what you do.
- Your natural creative and intellectual talents — because forcing yourself into roles that don't suit you will never create sustainable wealth.
- Your personal lifestyle goals — because wealth should support your freedom, not take it away.

A business should work for you, not consume you.

This means:

- Choosing hours that suit you instead of grinding yourself into exhaustion.
- Leveraging systems, platforms, and automation to scale your success without overworking.
- Creating a structure that allows you to thrive personally and financially.

The goal is not just to make money — it is to create a business that supports your highest vision for your life.

The Power of Leverage: Work Smarter, Not Harder

The biggest difference between those who struggle financially and those who thrive is how they use leverage.

- Traditional work model = Trading time for money in a linear way
- The *Fast-Track Millionairess* model = Using leverage to multiply impact and income

Fast-Track Millionairess

Leverage means:

- Using technology and automation to create passive or scalable income
- Building systems that do the work for you instead of being stuck in manual labor
- Licensing, digital products, and memberships that allow you to earn while you sleep
- Strategic collaborations that help you reach more people with less effort

The wealthiest women do not work harder. They use smarter systems, platforms, and structures to create financial expansion while maintaining personal freedom.

Solving Problems That Create Transformation

Money flows to those who solve problems.

If you want to build lasting wealth, your focus should not be on "making money" but on identifying problems and creating solutions that help people transform.

- People do not pay for products or services. They pay for results, relief, and transformation.
- The fastest way to financial success is to find a group of people with a pressing problem and create a solution that improves their lives.
- The bigger the problem you solve, the greater the financial reward.

Instead of asking, How can I make more money? Shift to:

- What do people deeply need that I can help with?
- How can I use my knowledge, creativity, or experience to make their lives better?
- How can I build something that truly serves others in a meaningful way?

Money follows impact. When you focus on creating genuine value, financial success is inevitable.

Removing Self-Worth from the Equation — Serve Without Sacrificing Yourself

Many women struggle to charge for their work because they tie their prices to their self-worth.

But this is a mistake.

- Your worth as a person is infinite. It cannot be measured in money.
- The price of your services should reflect the value of the transformation you provide, not how you feel about yourself.
- Charging market rates is not about "proving" yourself — it is about setting an exchange that allows you to sustain and grow.

Wealth is not built through over-giving, undercharging, or feeling guilty for success.

The *Fast-Track Millionairess* model is about:

- Serving powerfully, not sacrificing endlessly.
- Setting clear boundaries on what you will and won't do.
- Valuing your time, energy, and expertise — and expecting others to do the same.

You are not obligated to give away your talents for free. The world needs women who are thriving, not women who are drained, depleted, and resentful.

Creating a Community That Thrives Together

True wealth is not built in isolation.

The most powerful and financially successful women are community builders. They:

- Lift others up instead of competing.

- Create spaces where people feel supported, seen, and empowered.
- Surround themselves with people who are also committed to growth.

Wealth is not just about money — it is about creating networks, alliances, and opportunities that allow everyone to rise together.

The more you build people up, the more wealth flows into your life.

Charging Your Worth and Attracting the Right Audience

- You do not need to convince the wrong people to value you. You need to find the people who already align with what you offer.
- Charging market rates is not about greed — it is about sustainability. If you undervalue yourself, you will not have the energy or resources to keep growing.
- You do not need to appeal to everyone. Focus on finding the audience that resonates with you, thrives with you, and is excited to invest in what you offer.

Money flows to those who:

- Know their value and charge accordingly
- Find the right people instead of chasing uninterested ones
- Deliver results and transformation with confidence

The wealthiest women are not afraid to charge. They know that what they offer is worth every penny.

The *Fast-Track Millionairess* Wealth Formula

- **You are not here to work for someone else's dream** — you are here to build your own.
- **Trading time for money is not the only way** — use leverage, systems, and creativity to expand your income.

- **Wealth follows problem-solving**. If you create transformation, you will never lack money.
- **Your self-worth is not up for debate** — set clear boundaries, charge market rates, and serve without sacrificing.
- **Money flows to those who build people up**, create value, and take full ownership of their potential.

When you stop waiting, playing small, and doubting yourself — and start owning your skills, serving at a high level, and stepping into leadership — you unlock wealth on your terms.

Because true wealth is not just about making money.

It is about building a life of freedom, purpose, and limitless expansion.

Key income streams

Most people think about income in one-dimensional terms — what they earn from their job or profession. They define themselves by their title — *accountant, artist, healer, consultant* — and limit their earning potential to what that role allows.

But true financial expansion begins when you stop thinking of yourself in terms of a title and start recognizing yourself as a soul with a lifetime of experiences, talents, and skills.

When you view yourself only as your profession, you box yourself in, restricting your potential to what that title allows. But when you acknowledge that you are a multi-dimensional being with a unique combination of experiences, knowledge, and creativity, you realize that your income potential is limitless.

Your titles simply give credibility to your talents — but they are not your entire value.

The moment you shift from defining yourself by what you do to embracing all that you are, you unlock new pathways for wealth.

Fast-Track Millionairess

The Limits of Traditional Employment: Why Jobs Keep People Stuck

For many people, a job is their only source of income. It provides a sense of security, but it also comes with significant limitations:

- Your income is capped — No matter how hard you work, there is a limit to how much you can earn. Raises and promotions depend on company budgets, policies, and often the subjective opinions of managers.
- You are at the mercy of others for career growth — Your progress is not based solely on merit. It is influenced by workplace politics, relationships, favoritism, and opportunities that may or may not be given to you.
- You are replaceable — No matter how valuable you are, a company can decide to restructure, downsize, or replace you at any time.
- There is a glass ceiling on money and progression — Many industries have built-in limits on how far an individual can rise, particularly for women, minorities, and those who challenge the status quo.

No one should have the power to decide your financial future but you.

If you depend solely on a job for income, you are placing your financial destiny in the hands of someone else.

This does not mean everyone should quit their jobs immediately — but it does mean that if you want true financial independence, you must start building income streams that are not controlled by someone else.

The Three Core Income Streams for a Millionairess

To create financial security and freedom, you must move beyond relying on only one source of income and develop a balance of income streams that support long-term wealth.

There are three primary paths to financial success:

- 1. Business Income (Active and Scalable Earnings)

- 2. Investments (Compounded Wealth Growth)
- 3. Passive Income (Leveraged and Automated Earnings)

1. Business Income — Monetizing Your Unique Value

Business is one of the most powerful ways to generate wealth because it allows you to leverage your experiences, skills, and creativity to create solutions for others.

You are not just your profession — you are a lifetime of insights, experiences, and talents.

To create business income, think beyond the limits of your job title and instead ask:

- *What problems can I help people solve using my knowledge and experiences?*
- *What skills do I have that people are willing to pay for?*
- *What transformation can I offer?*

Successful business income comes from creating value in the marketplace. The more people you help, the more money flows to you.

Some of the best business models for high-income potential include:

- Consulting and Coaching — Teaching others based on your expertise
- Online Courses and Programs — Turning knowledge into scalable digital products
- Service-Based Businesses — Offering solutions in health, finance, business, creativity, or personal development
- Product-Based Businesses — Selling physical or digital goods
- Community Building and Memberships — Creating spaces where people pay for access to your knowledge, resources, or network

Your experiences — no matter how unrelated they may seem — can be turned into business opportunities when positioned correctly.

Your business should reflect the full range of your gifts, not just the ones society has given you a title for.

2. Investments — Building Long-Term Wealth Growth

Most people believe that earning more money is the only way to get rich. But wealth is not just about how much you make — it's about how much you keep and grow.

Wealthy people don't just earn — they invest.

Investment income allows you to multiply your wealth over time, so money works for you even when you're not actively working.

Some of the most effective investment vehicles include:

- Stocks and Shares — Owning portions of companies that grow over time
- Real Estate — Creating long-term wealth through property ownership and rental income
- Index Funds and ETFs — Low-maintenance investment options for steady growth
- Cryptocurrency and Digital Assets — Newer investment classes with high-growth potential
- Angel Investing and Venture Capital — Funding startups in exchange for future returns
- Business Ownership and Partnerships — Investing in companies that generate passive income

Investing is not just for the ultra-wealthy — it is how ordinary people become financially free.

Fast-Track Millionairess

You do not need to start with large sums of money. Small, consistent investments — made wisely over time — compound into significant wealth.

3. Passive Income — Earning Without Constant Effort

Passive income is the ultimate key to financial freedom because it allows you to earn money without constantly trading your time for it.

Instead of working for every dollar, passive income streams are built once and continue to generate money.

Some of the most powerful passive income streams include:

- Royalties and Licensing — Earning from books, music, intellectual property, or creative works
- Affiliate Marketing — Earning commissions by recommending products
- Digital Products — Courses, ebooks, templates, or audio programs that sell automatically
- Subscription Models and Membership Sites — Recurring income from exclusive content or services
- Real Estate Rentals — Long-term passive cash flow through property investments
- Dividend Stocks and Interest-Bearing Accounts — Investments that generate regular returns

The secret to true wealth is moving from being the one who works for money to being the one who owns assets that generate money for you.

The *Fast-Track Millionairess* Income Formula

- **You are not just your job title** — you are a lifetime of experiences, skills, and creativity that can generate wealth in limitless ways.
- **Relying on one income stream is financial risk.** The wealthiest women diversify across business, investments, and passive income.

- **Working for others means your earning potential is controlled by someone else.** To gain financial independence, you must build income streams you control.
- **Wealth creation is about leverage, not labor.** The goal is to move from working for money to having money work for you.
- **Your financial future is in your hands.** The moment you step out of limitation and into creation, wealth expansion becomes inevitable.

The wealthiest women are not the ones who rely on a job to define their income — they are the ones who take ownership of their financial destiny, create multiple pathways to wealth, and build businesses that align with their full range of gifts and experiences.

Breaking the Cycle of Trading Time for Money

For most of the world, money is directly linked to time. You work a set number of hours, and you receive a set amount of pay. This is the default financial model — whether you are an employee earning a salary or a freelancer charging by the hour.

But this system has a fundamental flaw: There are only so many hours in a day.

- If your income is tied to your time, your earning potential is automatically capped.
- If you want to earn more, you have to work more hours — which leads to burnout, exhaustion, and limited financial freedom.
- If you stop working, the income stops too — meaning you are always at risk of financial instability.

This time-for-money trap is why so many people — even high earners — stay stuck in financial stress.

The *Fast-Track Millionairess* model is about breaking this cycle completely.

Fast-Track Millionairess

Instead of making money based on time, you must learn to make money based on value, systems, and leverage.

The Problem with the Time-for-Money Model

Most people believe that if they want to make more money, they need to:

- Work longer hours
- Take on more clients
- Get a higher-paying job

But all of these solutions still rely on exchanging time for money — which means:

- Your income is always dependent on how much you work — there is no room for real freedom.
- There is no scalability — if you are the only one generating income, your earnings are always limited by your availability.
- Burnout is inevitable — the harder you work, the more exhausted you become, leading to diminishing returns.

No matter how much you love your work, trading time for money is not sustainable long-term.

The wealthiest people in the world do not work more hours than everyone else.

They work differently. They leverage systems that allow them to earn without being physically present every minute of the day.

How to Break Free from the Time-for-Money Trap

To shift from working harder to earning smarter, you must change the way you think about income.

Instead of asking, *How can I work more to make more money?*, ask:

- How can I create value that generates money without requiring constant effort?
- How can I build systems that continue making money even when I'm not actively working?
- How can I leverage my skills, knowledge, and creativity to earn in multiple ways?

The goal is to decouple your income from your time — so that you can earn money in ways that do not require constant labor.

Here's how to start:

Create Scalable Income Streams

Scalability means that your income can grow without increasing your workload.

Traditional jobs and hourly services are not scalable because they require direct effort for every dollar earned.

Instead, shift to income streams that allow one action to generate multiple sales or clients without extra effort.

Examples include:

- Digital Products — Courses, ebooks, templates, or masterclasses that can be sold repeatedly without additional work.
- Group Coaching and Programs — Serving multiple people at once instead of one-on-one work.
- Subscription and Membership Models — Recurring income from communities, exclusive content, or ongoing services.
- Affiliate Marketing — Earning commissions by recommending valuable products or services.
- Licensing and Royalties — Creating intellectual property that others can pay to use.

Instead of being paid per hour, start creating ways to be paid per solution.

Leverage Systems and Automation

If your business relies on you to personally handle every task, you have created another job for yourself — not financial freedom.

The wealthiest business owners are not the ones doing everything themselves — they are the ones who leverage systems to multiply their income.

Some of the best automation tools include:

- Sales Funnels — Automated sequences that generate leads and convert sales without your direct involvement.
- Email Marketing — Pre-written emails that build relationships and sell your products or services while you sleep.
- Social Media Scheduling — Automating content so that your brand grows even when you're offline.
- Outsourcing and Delegation — Hiring team members or freelancers to take over repetitive tasks.

Wealth is not built by doing everything yourself — it is built by creating systems that generate income for you.

Use Investment Income to Build Long-Term Wealth

Wealthy people do not just earn money — they make their money work for them.

Even if you have a high-income business, true financial independence comes when your money continues growing without your active involvement.

Some of the best ways to build self-sustaining wealth include:

- Stock Market Investments — Dividends and market growth that compound over time.

- Real Estate Rentals — Properties that generate monthly passive income.
- Business Investments — Owning shares in companies that grow in value.

This is how the rich get richer — by using money to make more money.

If your money is not working for you, you will always be working for money.

Charge for Results, Not Time

Most people underprice themselves because they charge based on effort rather than outcome.

If you are delivering high-value results, you should be charging for the transformation, not for the time it takes you to deliver it.

For example:

- If a financial coach helps someone save £50,000 in one year, should they only charge for the hours they worked? Or should they charge for the life-changing result?
- If a business strategist helps a company double its revenue, should they charge per hour or based on the impact of their work?
- If a healer helps someone regain their energy and confidence, is the value only in the time spent together, or in the lasting change created?

Wealth is built by charging for value, not for effort.

Stop pricing yourself based on time. Start charging based on the transformation you create.

Build Income Streams That Work While You Rest

The ultimate goal is financial security that does not rely on constant work.

If you had to stop working tomorrow, would your income stop too?

Fast-Track Millionairess

If the answer is yes, your finances are still in the time-for-money trap.

To truly break free, start building income streams that generate money even when you're offline.

The moment you have money coming in while you sleep, you have escaped the rat race.

The Fast-Track Millionairess Wealth Formula

- **Money should not be tied to time** — it should be tied to value.
- **Trading time for money keeps you limited** — leveraging systems creates unlimited income potential.
- **Automation, scalable products, and investments** are the key to financial independence.
- **Wealthy people don't work harder** — they create assets that generate money for them.
- **If your income stops when you stop working**, you are not financially free yet.

To step into financial independence, you must unlearn the idea that wealth comes from effort alone.

Wealth is built by creating, leveraging, and scaling income — not by working longer hours.

The moment you stop trading time for money and start building income streams that work for you, you step into true financial power.

Chapter 6: Digital Empire — How to Make Money Online Without Burnout

The Best Business Models for Women Who Want Freedom

The digital world has completely transformed the way wealth is created. Women no longer have to choose between financial success and personal freedom — they can have both by building businesses that align with their energy, creativity, and lifestyle goals.

But not all business models support freedom. Many online businesses are structured in a way that traps women in another version of the rat race — constantly chasing clients, creating content at unsustainable levels, or working around the clock just to keep things going.

The key to true financial and time freedom is choosing a business model that:

- Leverages your unique talents and strengths
- Allows you to work on your own terms
- Has scalable and passive income potential
- Aligns with your energy cycles instead of forcing you into burnout

Success is not just about making money — it's about creating a business that enhances your life, not drains it.

Here are the best business models for women who want freedom, flexibility, and financial independence.

Digital Products and Online Courses

Best for: Women who love teaching, coaching, or sharing knowledge

One of the fastest-growing ways to build a profitable and scalable online business is through digital products. This includes:

- Online courses — Teaching skills, knowledge, or expertise through structured programs
- Ebooks and guides — Downloadable content that provides valuable information
- Workbooks and templates — Pre-designed frameworks that help people solve specific problems
- Membership sites — Exclusive content and training for subscribers

Why it works:

- Unlimited earning potential — You create it once and sell it repeatedly.
- Scalable — Unlike coaching or consulting, where you are limited by time, digital products generate income without constant effort.
- Passive income — Once set up, you can earn from sales while you sleep.

Instead of trading time for money, you are leveraging knowledge for money.

Coaching, Consulting and Mentorship

Best for: Women who want to help others through guidance, transformation, or expertise

If you have knowledge, experience, or a unique skill set, coaching and consulting can be a highly lucrative business model.

This can include:

- One-on-one coaching — Personalized guidance for clients in any niche (business, wellness, relationships, mindset, career, etc.).
- Group coaching programs — Helping multiple people at once, increasing income while reducing time spent.
- High-ticket consulting — Offering specialized expertise to businesses or individuals.

Fast-Track Millionairess

Why it works:

- You can charge premium rates — Because people pay for transformation, not just time.
- It allows for deep impact — Helping people achieve significant changes in their lives or businesses.
- You can scale it — By transitioning from one-on-one to group coaching or digital programs.

You don't need a certification — your experience, wisdom, and ability to create results are what matter most.

Subscription and Membership Models

Best for: Women who want recurring, predictable income

A membership or subscription business creates ongoing income instead of one-time sales. Examples include:

- Exclusive content communities — Paid private groups, masterminds, or mentorship spaces
- Monthly resource libraries — Providing templates, meditations, tools, or training videos
- Continuity programs — Ongoing coaching, learning, or networking opportunities

Why it works:

- Predictable monthly income — Stability instead of feast-or-famine income cycles.
- Loyal community building — You nurture relationships with members long-term.
- Low-maintenance once established — You provide ongoing value but aren't constantly chasing new customers.

Fast-Track Millionairess

This model is perfect for women who want steady income with lower marketing pressure.

Affiliate Marketing and Brand Partnerships

Best for: Women who want income without creating their own products

Affiliate marketing allows you to earn commission-based income by promoting other people's products or services.

This can include:

- Recommending tools, courses, or services
- Creating content that includes affiliate links
- Working with brands on sponsored partnerships

Why it works:

- No product creation needed — You don't need to develop your own offers.
- Works well with content creation — If you already have a blog, YouTube channel, or social media presence, it's an easy way to monetize.
- Passive income potential — Once links are in place, commissions can flow in consistently.

If you naturally recommend products you love, affiliate marketing can be an easy income stream.

Content Monetization (YouTube, Podcasting, Blogging)

Best for: Women who love creating content and sharing their voice

Building a personal brand through content creation is one of the most powerful ways to attract opportunities, clients, and income streams.

Fast-Track Millionairess

Options include:

- YouTube channel monetization (ads, sponsorships, memberships)
- Podcast sponsorships (getting paid to feature brands)
- Blogging with ad revenue and affiliate links
- Social media brand deals and collaborations

Why it works:

- You build an engaged audience that trusts you — which opens up multiple income opportunities.
- You own your platform — Unlike relying on social media algorithms, a blog, podcast, or YouTube channel is a long-term asset.
- It allows for multiple streams of income — Affiliate marketing, brand deals, courses, and services can all flow from content.

Your voice and message can be turned into a business that makes money while you create impact.

E-commerce and Digital Shops

Best for: Women who want to sell physical or digital products

With platforms like Shopify, Etsy, and Amazon, starting an online store has never been easier.

Product ideas include:

- Physical products (handmade goods, print-on-demand clothing, unique items)
- Digital products (printables, planners, stock photos, online tools)
- Dropshipping and white labeling (selling products without handling inventory)

Fast-Track Millionairess

Why it works:

- Low startup costs with digital products — You create once and sell infinitely.
- E-commerce automation — With the right setup, stores can generate income with minimal hands-on effort.
- Passive potential — Once optimized, products can sell without active promotion.

If you love product creation, e-commerce can be a powerful wealth-building tool.

Choosing the Right Business Model for YOU

The best business model is not the one that makes the most money — it is the one that aligns with:

- Your natural strengths and passions
- Your desired lifestyle and working style
- Your energy levels and preferred way of creating value

Questions to ask yourself:

- Do I enjoy creating digital content, or do I prefer working directly with people?
- Do I want to create my own products, or would I rather sell existing ones?
- Do I want recurring income, or do I prefer one-time high-ticket sales?
- How much time do I want to spend actively working vs. earning passively?

The beauty of the digital business landscape is that you do not have to choose just one income stream — you can layer multiple models together over time.

For example:

- A coach can sell digital courses and a membership.

- A content creator can monetize YouTube, offer affiliate links, and launch a product line.
- A consultant can build a scalable group program while investing profits into real estate.

Freedom comes from designing a business that works for YOU — not forcing yourself into someone else's formula for success.

The *Fast-Track Millionairess* Digital Business Formula

- **The best business model** supports both financial success and personal freedom.
- **Online income is limitless** — but only if you create systems that allow for scalability.
- **Not all business models align with every woman** — choose what feels best for YOU.
- **Layering multiple income streams over time** creates long-term security.
- **The key to digital wealth is alignment** — when you build a business that fits your energy, money flows effortlessly.

The right online business is the one that gives you the income, impact, and lifestyle you desire — without burnout.

The Power of Youtube, Courses, and Coaching

In the digital world, the three most powerful business models for women who want freedom, impact, and financial success are:

- YouTube (content creation and audience building)
- Online courses (scalable knowledge-sharing)
- Coaching (high-impact transformation for individuals and groups)

Each of these models leverages your expertise, creativity, and ability to serve others, while allowing you to step away from trading time for money.

The secret to digital wealth is not just making money — it's creating assets that grow in value over time.

Let's break down why these three business models are so powerful and how they work together to create a high-income, high-freedom digital empire.

YouTube: The Ultimate Business Growth Tool

YouTube is one of the most powerful wealth-building platforms available today. Unlike social media platforms that bury your content within hours, YouTube videos remain searchable and continue generating traffic for years.

Why YouTube is the Perfect Foundation for an Online Business

Evergreen content = long-term income: A well-made video can bring in views, subscribers, and revenue for years after posting.

Global reach without paid ads: Unlike traditional advertising, YouTube allows you to reach thousands — even millions — of people organically.

Multiple monetization options: YouTube is not just about ad revenue. You can earn from:

- YouTube Partner Program: YouTube runs ads on its videos and rewards content creators with a share of the ad revenue.
- Affiliate marketing: Recommending products and earning commissions
- Sponsorships: Brands paying to feature their products in your videos
- Selling your own courses, coaching, or digital products

How to Use YouTube to Grow Your Business

Position yourself as an expert — Share valuable insights, knowledge, or entertaining content in your niche.

- Use videos to lead into paid offers — Create free content that naturally guides people to your courses, coaching, or products.
- Build a loyal audience — Subscribers trust and connect with you, making them more likely to buy from you.
- Make content once, get paid forever — Unlike social media posts that disappear, a great video keeps working for you indefinitely.

YouTube allows you to serve thousands of people at once — without needing to be present in real-time.

Online Courses: The Best Way to Scale Your Knowledge

An online course is a structured way to package and sell your expertise, allowing you to help people at scale without needing to work with them one-on-one.

Courses are one of the fastest ways to go from active income to passive income, because once they are created, they can be sold without requiring additional effort.

Why Online Courses Are So Powerful

You create it once, but sell it infinitely: Unlike coaching, where you work with one person at a time, courses allow you to teach hundreds (or thousands) of people at once.

Higher perceived value = higher income potential: People pay more for structured, transformational learning experiences than they do for casual content.

Low maintenance income stream: Once your course is built, your primary focus is marketing and scaling, rather than constantly delivering content.

Creates an asset that increases in value over time: As you refine and update your course, it becomes even more valuable, allowing you to charge premium prices.

Fast-Track Millionairess

How to Use Courses to Generate Income

Identify a transformation you can offer — What can you teach that helps someone achieve a goal or solve a problem?

- Package your knowledge into an engaging format — Videos, PDFs, templates, and exercises.
- Market through YouTube, email, and social media — Use content to attract ideal students.
- Sell at multiple price points — Create mini-courses, high-ticket programs, or tiered learning experiences.

Courses allow you to earn like a teacher — but with no limit on how many "students" you can serve at once.

Coaching: The Most Direct Path to High-Income Impact

Coaching is the fastest way to create a profitable online business because it allows you to:

- Charge premium rates for your time and expertise
- Help clients get real transformation and results
- Work in high-touch, high-impact ways that deepen your client relationships

Why Coaching is a Powerful Business Model

You can start immediately — Unlike courses, which require content creation, coaching simply requires your knowledge and willingness to guide people.

High-income potential — Many coaches charge $1,000–$10,000+ per client for transformational coaching packages.

Helps you refine your expertise — Coaching deepens your understanding of what people truly need, making it easier to create even better courses and content.

Easiest business model to launch — No tech skills required — just the ability to help others succeed.

Types of Coaching Models

- One-on-One Coaching — Personalized, high-ticket services
- Group Coaching — Helping multiple clients at once (scaling your income while reducing time commitment)
- Hybrid Programs — Combining coaching with digital courses or memberships for a multi-tiered business model

Coaching is the fastest way to monetize your expertise — while directly impacting people's lives.

The Power of Combining YouTube, Courses, and Coaching

These three business models work together to create a powerful, self-sustaining ecosystem:

Youtube Builds Trust and Attracts Your Ideal Audience

Viewers get to know you, your expertise, and your teaching style for free.

Some will watch your content and want more — leading them to your paid offers.

Courses Provide Passive Income and Scale Your Impact

Instead of repeating the same lessons for individual clients, your course teaches once and sells infinitely.

This allows you to help more people without exhausting yourself.

Coaching Deepens Transformation and Increases Revenue

Some students will want more personal guidance — leading them to your coaching programs.

Fast-Track Millionairess

High-ticket coaching creates fast, high-profit income streams that fund long-term business growth.

This combination allows you to:

- Attract clients effortlessly through YouTube with no paid advertising costs required.
- Scale your income with courses instead of being limited by your time.
- Charge premium rates for deep transformation in coaching creating a high-end revenue stream.

This is how women build multi-six and seven-figure businesses online — without burnout.

The *Fast-Track Millionairess* Digital Business Formula

- **YouTube is the ultimate audience-building machine** — giving you visibility, trust, and passive income.
- **Online courses allow you to scale knowledge into wealth** — teaching once and earning infinitely.
- **Coaching creates deep transformation** and premium-level income.
- **The most successful online businesses** combine all three for maximum impact and freedom.
- **Wealth is built by aligning** your expertise with scalable, high-value offers.

You do not have to choose between money and freedom. The right business model allows you to have both.

Leveraging Automation and Passive Income Streams

For too long, women have been taught that hard work equals financial success — that to earn more, they must work longer hours, take on more clients, and push themselves to exhaustion.

But wealth is not built by working harder — it is built by working smarter.

Fast-Track Millionairess

The women who create true financial freedom are not the ones who grind endlessly; they are the ones who build systems that make money flow to them automatically.

This is where automation and passive income become game-changers.

When you stop relying on direct effort for every dollar earned, you step into a business model that supports both wealth and freedom.

Why Automation and Passive Income Are Essential

Most people stay trapped in active income — where they must work in order to earn.

- If they stop working, their income stops.
- If they get sick or take time off, they lose money.
- If they want to scale, they must work more hours.

This creates a constant cycle of stress and burnout.

Passive income and automation break this cycle by creating income streams that continue generating money even when you are not actively working.

The goal is not just to make more money — it is to build systems that free you from the need to constantly "hustle."

Automating Your Business for Scalable Growth

Automation allows you to serve more people, sell more products, and generate more revenue — without increasing your workload.

Instead of manually doing everything, you set up systems that work for you in the background.

Some of the best ways to automate an online business include:

Sales Funnels and Email Marketing

Instead of manually selling your products or services, automate the process with a sales funnel.

A sales funnel is a step-by-step journey that leads potential clients from interest to purchase — without requiring you to personally sell to each individual.

Automated email sequences nurture your audience, build trust, and guide them toward buying — even while you sleep.

Once set up, your emails continue working for you — turning visitors into customers automatically.

Pre-Scheduled Content and Social Media Automation

Posting content manually every day is exhausting and unsustainable.

Use scheduling tools to batch-create content and automate posting across platforms.

This keeps your audience engaged without requiring daily effort.

Your business continues growing even when you take a break.

Chatbots and Customer Support Automation

If you get a lot of the same questions, automate responses with AI-driven chatbots or FAQ sections.

Use automated booking systems for coaching calls or consultations.

Set up pre-recorded webinars to generate sales on autopilot.

This removes repetitive tasks and allows you to focus on growth instead of admin work.

Fast-Track Millionairess

Creating Passive Income Streams That Work for You

Passive income means you create something once, and it continues to generate money.

Instead of constantly chasing clients or working for every dollar, you set up long-term revenue streams that provide financial stability and freedom.

Digital Products and Online Courses

Instead of trading time for money, turn your expertise into an asset.

Sell courses, ebooks, templates, or masterclasses that people can purchase anytime — without you having to be there.

Platforms like Kajabi, Teachable, and Thinkific allow you to sell knowledge as a product.

The key to passive income is creating something once that keeps selling indefinitely.

Membership Sites and Subscription Models

Instead of one-time purchases, create a recurring income stream.

Offer exclusive content, group coaching, or ongoing training inside a monthly membership or subscription.

This provides predictable, consistent revenue each month.

This is perfect for building community while creating stable income.

Affiliate Marketing and Brand Partnerships

Instead of creating all your own products, earn commissions by promoting products you love.

Recommend tools, courses, or services and earn a percentage of each sale.

You can do this through blog posts, YouTube videos, or email marketing.

You get paid for sharing valuable recommendations — without handling the product or customer service.

YouTube and Content Monetization

YouTube videos continue generating ad revenue long after they are posted.

Monetize your channel through:

- Ad revenue (YouTube Partner Program)
- Sponsorship deals (brands paying for product placements)
- Affiliate links in descriptions (earning commissions from recommendations)

A well-made YouTube video can generate income for years.

Content is an asset that keeps paying you — even long after you create it.

Investments and Financial Passive Income

Use profits from your business to invest in stocks, real estate, or high-yield assets.

Dividend stocks, rental properties, or interest-bearing accounts allow you to earn money without active effort.

This ensures your money continues growing, even if your business slows down.

Wealthy people do not just earn — they invest. Let your money work for you.

How to Structure a Business That Runs Itself

The ultimate goal is to shift from a business that requires constant effort to one that generates revenue automatically.

Fast-Track Millionairess

To do this, follow a three-phase strategy:

Phase 1: Build Your Core Business and Revenue Stream

- Launch a service-based or knowledge-based business (coaching, consulting, courses).
- Focus on one core income stream at first.
- Build brand trust through content marketing, YouTube, or social media.

Phase 2: Automate and Scale

- Create an evergreen product (course, digital download, membership).
- Set up automated sales funnels and email sequences to sell consistently.
- Use ads, SEO, or organic traffic to drive people into your funnel.

Phase 3: Add Passive Income Streams

- Introduce investments, real estate, and financial passive income.
- Increase automated revenue sources (affiliates, YouTube, content monetization).
- Focus on high-impact growth, not daily tasks.

The goal is to transition from "doing" to "owning" — where your business becomes an income-producing asset, not just a job.

The *Fast-Track Millionairess* Passive Income Formula

- **Money should not stop when you stop working.** Build systems that generate income even when you take time off.
- **Automation is not optional — it is the key to sustainable success.** If you are doing repetitive tasks manually, you are holding back your growth.
- **Passive income is not about doing nothing** — it is about setting up systems that work without constant effort.
- **Your business should serve YOU — not the other way around.** The right systems create wealth while protecting your energy.

- **The wealthiest women do not work more hours** — they own assets that generate money for them.

When you master automation and passive income, you no longer work for money — money works for you.

Doing What You Love and Getting Paid for It

For generations, women have been told they must choose between passion and profit — that doing what they love is a luxury, not a viable way to make money.

This belief has kept countless women stuck in jobs they hate, trading their time for a paycheck while their true talents and dreams remain untapped.

But the reality is this:

The most successful and fulfilled people in the world are those who do what they love — and get paid extremely well for it.

The key is not just following your passion blindly but learning how to monetize it strategically, align it with market demand, and create multiple income streams that support it.

The Myth of the "Starving Artist" (and Why It's Completely False)

Many women hesitate to pursue their passions because they have been conditioned to believe that certain careers are "unstable" or that making money from creativity, healing, or personal growth is unrealistic.

But this is a deeply outdated belief.

Every industry has people who are thriving. There are wealthy artists, musicians, coaches, writers, and healers — just as there are struggling professionals in traditional careers.

Fast-Track Millionairess

The online world has created limitless opportunities. With digital platforms, automation, and global audiences, any skill, talent, or passion can be monetized.

Wealth follows value, not effort. The question is not *Can I make money doing what I love?* It's *How can I structure it in a way that creates real value for others?*

You don't have to choose between passion and financial success — you just need to learn how to align the two.

Turning Your Passion into a Profitable Business

If you want to get paid for doing what you love, you need to shift from seeing it as just a passion to seeing it as an opportunity to create transformation for others.

Here's how:

Identify Your Passion and Strengths

- What do you love doing that comes naturally to you?
- What are people always asking for your advice or help with?
- What activities make you feel the most alive?

The things you do effortlessly are often where your greatest financial opportunities lie.

Find the Intersection of Passion and Market Demand

Passion alone is not enough — you need to connect it to something that solves a problem or fulfills a need.

Ask: *How does my passion help others? How does it create a transformation?*

Research industries where people are already paying for what you love to do.

The fastest way to monetize your passion is to solve a real problem with it.

Fast-Track Millionairess

Choose the Right Business Model for Your Passion

Depending on your passion, different business models will suit you best:

- If you love teaching → Create online courses, workshops, or coaching programs.
- If you love creating → Sell digital products, art, books, or handmade goods.
- If you love inspiring others → Build a brand on YouTube, blogging, or podcasting.
- If you love healing and guiding → Offer private sessions, memberships, or transformational programs.

There is always a way to monetize your gifts — you just need to package them correctly.

Stop Trading Time for Money — Create Scalable Income Streams

Instead of relying only on hourly work or one-on-one sessions, build scalable income.

Example: A yoga instructor can teach private sessions, but they can also create an online yoga course or a membership program.

The goal is to build assets that work for you, not just with you.

Passive and leveraged income ensure you never feel trapped by your own business.

Charge for the Value, Not the Time

Women often undercharge because they tie their prices to their self-worth — instead, price based on the transformation you provide.

If you help someone save time, make money, heal, or improve their life, you are creating value — and value is worth money.

Fast-Track Millionairess

The wealthiest people do not get paid for effort — they get paid for results.

Charge based on impact, not on how long something takes you to create.

Monetizing Your Passion Without Burnout

The key to sustainable success is doing what you love in a way that protects your energy and allows you to scale.

To avoid burnout while building wealth:

- Set boundaries — Just because you love it doesn't mean you should do it 24/7 for free.
- Leverage systems and automation — Create passive income streams so your business runs even when you're not actively working.
- Charge appropriately — If you undercharge, you will exhaust yourself trying to make ends meet.
- Learn marketing and sales — Talent alone is not enough — success comes from knowing how to position and sell your work.
- Find your ideal audience — Stop trying to convince the wrong people to value you; instead, attract the right people who already do.

Passion should feel energizing, not exhausting. Build in a way that supports both your creativity and your well-being.

Why Doing What You Love Is the Fastest Path to Wealth

When you align your natural talents, passions, and business model, something powerful happens:

- You become magnetic. People can feel when you are doing something you love, and they are naturally drawn to that energy.
- You create at a higher level. When you love your work, you are constantly inspired, which leads to greater innovation and success.

Fast-Track Millionairess

- You attract the right opportunities. Wealth is easier to build when you are aligned with your purpose, rather than forcing yourself into work that drains you.
- You sustain long-term success. You are far less likely to burn out when you are building a business that excites and nourishes you.

Passion-driven businesses last longer because they are fueled by inspiration, not just obligation.

The Fast-Track Millionairess Passion Formula

- **You do not have to choose between passion and money** — you can have both.
- **Monetizing a passion** is about solving problems and creating transformation for others.
- **Doing what you love should bring wealth, not burnout** — choose scalable business models that allow you to grow sustainably.
- **Charge based on value, not time** — your impact is what people pay for.
- **The most successful businesses are built on alignment** — when you love your work, success follows naturally.

You are not here to work a job you hate. You are here to create, inspire, and build wealth by doing what sets your soul on fire.

Chapter 7: The Pricing Revolution — How to Charge What You're Worth

The Fear of Pricing and How to Overcome It

Pricing is one of the biggest struggles for women in business.

No matter how skilled, experienced, or talented they are, many women hesitate to charge their worth — and even when they do, they often feel guilt, fear, or anxiety about it.

Why? Because pricing is not just about numbers — it is about self-worth, confidence, and the belief that what you offer has value.

Your pricing is a reflection of how much you believe in your own impact.

The truth is, pricing fear is not logical — it is emotional.

And if you do not learn to overcome it, you will:

- Undercharge and overwork, leading to burnout.
- Struggle to grow because your business won't be profitable.
- Resent your work because you are not being properly compensated for it.

This is why pricing is not just a financial decision — it is a mindset shift.

Why Women Struggle to Charge Their Worth

Women's struggles with pricing are deeply ingrained in social conditioning, fear of rejection, and a misunderstanding of value.

Some of the biggest pricing fears include:

Fast-Track Millionairess

What if people can't afford me?

Many women price based on what they think people can pay, rather than on the value they provide.

Reality check: There is a market at every price point. If some people can't afford you, they are not your audience.

Your job is not to make your pricing "affordable" for everyone — it is to find the right people who see the value in what you offer.

I feel guilty charging for something I love doing.

Women are often conditioned to give away their gifts for free — especially in fields like healing, coaching, and creativity.

Reality check: Passion does not mean free labor. Doctors love medicine, but they charge. Artists love creating, but they sell.

Loving your work is a gift, but it does not mean you shouldn't be paid for it.

What if people say I'm too expensive?

Fear of rejection is one of the biggest blocks to raising prices.

Reality check: The right people will always pay for transformation. If someone says you are too expensive, it means they are not a good fit.

You do not need to justify your prices — stand by them with confidence.

I don't feel qualified enough to charge more.

Women often feel they need more certifications, experience, or validation before raising their prices.

Reality check: People do not pay for certificates — they pay for results. If you can help them, you are worth every penny.

Fast-Track Millionairess

Stop waiting for permission to charge more — own your value now.

What if I lose clients by charging more?

Many women fear that increasing their prices will drive clients away.

Reality check: When you charge more, you attract higher-quality clients who are serious about transformation.

Undercharging attracts people who do not value your work — raising prices attracts those who do.

How to Overcome Pricing Fear and Step into Confidence

Fear around pricing will not disappear overnight, but you can rewire your mindset to charge with confidence.

Stop Making Pricing Personal

Pricing is a business decision, not a personal reflection of your worth.

Charge based on market value, demand, and the transformation you provide — not based on how you feel about yourself.

Your worth is infinite — your pricing is simply an exchange of value.

Anchor Your Prices in Transformation

People do not buy your time, effort, or background — they buy the results you provide.

Ask yourself: What is the outcome of my work worth to my client?

If your service helps someone make more money, find love, heal, grow, or transform their life, it is worth charging for.

People are not paying for you — they are paying for their own transformation through your expertise.

Understand That Price Reflects Perceived Value

Lower prices often make people doubt the quality of what you offer.

When you price confidently, you signal that your work is valuable, high-quality, and worth investing in.

Studies show that people who pay more commit more, value more, and get better results.

Underpricing hurts both you and your clients — pricing correctly leads to stronger results for everyone.

Practice Saying Your Prices Without Hesitation

If you stutter, apologize, or explain your prices, it shows insecurity.

The more confidently you state your prices, the easier it is for clients to accept them.

Your pricing energy sets the tone — if you believe in it, others will too.

Charge What You Want — Then Add Tax

Many women automatically lower their prices to what feels "comfortable."

Instead, set the price you actually want to charge — then increase it by 20%.

This pushes you outside your comfort zone and ensures you are not undervaluing yourself.

If your pricing feels too easy to say, it is probably too low.

Fast-Track Millionairess

The *Fast-Track Millionairess* Pricing Formula

- **Pricing fear is not about money — it is about confidence.** When you believe in your value, pricing becomes easy.
- **You are not responsible for making your prices "affordable" for everyone** — your job is to find clients who align with your pricing.
- **People pay for results, not effort.** Charge based on the transformation you create, not the hours you put in.
- **Undercharging attracts low-value clients.** Raising prices attracts people who take your work seriously.
- **The moment you confidently own your prices**, you start attracting wealth effortlessly.

Fear will not disappear overnight, but the more you charge your worth, the more natural it becomes.

You are not just charging for your time — you are charging for:

- The years of experience it took to master your craft
- The unique insights and expertise you bring
- The life-changing results your clients receive
- The energy and care you put into each client's transformation

Your pricing is not a request — it is a statement of value.

Own your worth, set your price, and never apologize for it.

Why Women Undercharge and How to Break the Cycle

Women across industries — whether they are entrepreneurs, coaches, consultants, creatives, or service providers — consistently undercharge for their work. Even highly skilled, experienced women find themselves pricing far below their worth, leading to overwork, burnout, and frustration.

Undercharging is not just a pricing problem — it is a mindset and confidence issue.

The cycle of undercharging is deeply conditioned, but it is entirely possible to break free. Once you recognize why you have been pricing too low, you can start charging what you truly deserve — without hesitation or guilt.

Why Do Women Undercharge?

Women are often taught to devalue their own contributions, question their worth, and hesitate to ask for more. This conditioning runs deep, but it can be changed.

Here are the most common reasons women undercharge:

Social Conditioning to "Be Nice" and "Not Ask for Too Much"

From an early age, women are praised for being agreeable, helpful, and accommodating.

Many women are afraid of seeming greedy, demanding, or selfish when asking for more money.

They lower their prices to make people "like" them rather than pricing for financial sustainability.

Being underpaid does not make you kind — it makes you undervalued.

The Habit of Over-Giving Without Charging

Many women over-deliver for free — giving advice, coaching, support, or extra services without charging for it.

They believe that if they give enough for free, clients will eventually pay — but often, they just attract people who expect freebies.

When you give everything away for free, people assume your work has no value.

Tying Pricing to Self-Worth

Women often price their work based on their personal confidence level rather than the actual value of the transformation they provide.

If they feel insecure, they automatically lower their rates instead of focusing on the results they help others achieve.

Your pricing should be based on results, not on how you "feel" about yourself today.

Fear of Losing Clients

Many women set prices based on fear, thinking: "*If I charge too much, no one will buy.*" or "*I need to stay affordable so I don't scare people away.*"

This results in a low-ticket business model that forces them to work harder for less money.

You do not need to be "affordable" for everyone — your ideal clients will value and pay for your expertise.

Lack of Awareness of Industry Pricing Standards

Many women assume their prices are "fair" without actually researching what professionals in their industry charge.

They compare themselves to low-end competitors instead of aligning with top-tier professionals.

If you're pricing lower than market rates, you're positioning yourself as a beginner — even if you're highly skilled.

How to Break the Cycle of Undercharging

If you have been stuck in the undercharging trap, it's time to break free — permanently.

Here's how to shift your pricing mindset and confidently charge what you're worth:

Recognize That Pricing Is an Energy Exchange

Money is simply an exchange of energy — you are offering transformation, knowledge, and expertise.

If you undercharge, you create an imbalanced exchange where you give too much and receive too little.

Healthy pricing means you are being equally compensated for the energy, time, and results you deliver.

Stop Charging for Time — Start Charging for Transformation

People do not pay for your hours, your effort, or how hard you work.

They pay for the results you provide and the impact your work has on their life or business.

Your pricing should reflect the value of the transformation, not the time spent delivering it.

Align with Premium Pricing — Not Bargain Pricing

If you price yourself too low, people question your credibility and assume your work is lower quality.

High-value clients expect to invest at a premium level — they do not look for the cheapest option.

Fast-Track Millionairess

Instead of thinking, "How cheap can I make this?", start asking, "How valuable is this transformation?"

You will never attract high-value clients if you position yourself as a low-cost option.

Set Boundaries — No More Over-Giving

Stop giving away free advice, extra time, or emotional labor that should be paid for.

If you constantly over-deliver without charging, you will train people to expect more for less.

Your time, energy, and expertise are valuable — stop giving them away for free.

Use the "Double-Your-Price" Rule

If your current prices feel comfortable, double them.

If this feels scary, that's a sign that you were already undercharging.

If you never feel uncomfortable raising your rates, you're probably still undercharging.

Learn to Say Your Prices Without Apology

The way you deliver your price matters as much as the number itself.

Stop stuttering, apologizing, or explaining your prices — state them with confidence and silence.

The more confidently you say your price, the more people will accept it.

Let Go of Fear-Based Pricing

Raising your prices will not make you lose all your clients.

Fast-Track Millionairess

High-quality clients do not flinch at premium pricing — they expect it.

The only people who resist are those who were never going to invest seriously anyway.

If a client is only with you because you are the cheapest option, they are not the right client.

The *Fast-Track Millionairess* Pricing Formula

- **Undercharging is a habit** — not a reflection of your actual value.
- **You are not responsible for making your prices "affordable"** — you are responsible for delivering high-quality results.
- **Charging more attracts better clients** who take your work seriously.
- **Your pricing should be based on impact**, not personal insecurities.
- **When you confidently raise your rates,** you step into financial freedom.

Pricing is not about whether people "like" you — it is about creating a sustainable, abundant business that allows you to thrive.

The moment you break free from undercharging and start pricing based on value, you will:

- Work less while earning more.
- Attract high-level clients instead of bargain hunters.
- Build a business that supports your energy instead of draining it.

It is time to stop asking for less and start owning your worth.

Raise your prices. Stand by them. And never apologize for knowing your value.

The Psychology of High-Value Pricing

Most people assume pricing is just a number. But in reality, pricing is deeply psychological. It influences how people perceive value, how they make purchasing decisions, and how they commit to transformation.

Women, in particular, often price based on what feels "comfortable" rather than strategically using pricing to position themselves in the marketplace.

The most successful women in business understand that pricing is not just about covering costs — it is about signaling value, positioning authority, and attracting the right clients.

When you shift from low-cost pricing (which invites hesitation, doubt, and overwork) to high-value pricing (which creates authority, respect, and client commitment), your entire business transforms.

How Pricing Affects Perceived Value

Pricing is not just a financial decision — it is a trust factor.

When people see a higher price tag, they assume:

- The product or service must be more valuable.
- The provider must be highly skilled or experienced.
- The results must be better or more premium than lower-cost alternatives.

When people see a lower price tag, they assume:

- The quality must be lower.
- The provider must be less experienced or less confident.
- The results may not be as effective, exclusive, or premium.

People expect to pay more for things they trust — and they often distrust things that seem "too cheap."

Why Low Prices Can Hurt Your Business

Women often assume that keeping prices low will attract more clients, but in reality, low prices can repel the right clients and create unnecessary struggles.

Here's why:

Low Prices Attract More Hesitation, Not More Sales

When something is cheap, people doubt its value.

Instead of making a quick decision, they overthink, hesitate, and question whether it's worth it.

They ask for discounts, more details, or extra proof before buying.

Higher prices create instant confidence — people assume premium pricing means premium quality.

Low Prices Attract the Wrong Clients

Low-cost buyers are often the most difficult to work with — they expect more, complain more, and demand constant attention.

High-value clients respect your time and expertise — they invest fully and are more committed to results.

When you raise your prices, you upgrade the level of people you attract.

Cheap Pricing Creates a Cycle of Overwork

Charging too little means you have to take on more clients to make the same amount of money.

This leads to burnout, resentment, and exhaustion — instead of freedom and abundance.

Fast-Track Millionairess

High-value pricing allows you to work with fewer clients while making more money.

Why High-Value Pricing Works (The Luxury Mindset Shift)

Luxury brands and premium services use high-value pricing strategies because they understand how human psychology works.

People assume that if something is priced higher, it must be:

- Exclusive (not available to just anyone)
- Premium quality (better than cheaper alternatives)
- A smart investment (worth spending more on)

People do not question paying $5,000 for a luxury handbag — but they hesitate to spend $500 on self-improvement. Your job is to position your work as a premium investment, not an expense.

How to Position Yourself as a High-Value Expert

If you want to confidently charge premium prices, you must:

Shift from "Selling Services" to "Providing High-Value Transformation"

People do not pay for coaching, courses, or products — they pay for RESULTS.

Stop marketing your offer as a service — start framing it as a life-changing transformation.

People will pay any amount for something they truly believe will change their life or business.

Price for the Outcome, Not the Effort

Wrong thinking: "This only takes me 2 hours, so I should charge less."

Right thinking: *"This will change my client's life or business, so I should charge based on its impact."*

Example:

- If a consultant helps a business increase revenue by $100,000, should they only charge for the hours worked? Or should they charge for the massive value they created?
- If a healer helps a client release lifelong trauma, should they charge for the minutes of the session? Or should they price based on the transformation that will improve their entire life?

Price for the outcome, not the time it takes to deliver it.

Remove Money Blocks Around Charging More

Many women feel guilty about charging higher prices because they believe *"It's selfish to ask for more."*, *"I shouldn't make money from helping people."* or *"People might think I'm greedy."*

These are false money beliefs that must be rewritten.

The more money you earn, the more people you can help. Wealth allows you to serve at a higher level.

Use Pricing to Filter Out Low-Energy Clients

When you price too low, you invite people who:

- Hesitate, negotiate, and question everything
- Do not fully commit to the work
- Drain your energy instead of respecting your expertise

When you price at a high value, you attract people who:

- Take action immediately

- Are committed to their transformation
- Respect your boundaries and expertise

Premium pricing is not just about money — it is about working with people who are truly ready for the change you offer.

Confidently Communicate Your Prices

The way you say your price matters as much as the number itself.

If you hesitate, justify, or apologize for your prices, clients will doubt them too.

If you state them with confidence, clients will assume your prices are fair, justified, and worth it.

Your energy around pricing will dictate whether people accept it or question it.

The *Fast-Track Millionairess* High-Value Pricing Formula

- **People perceive higher prices as higher value** — use this to your advantage.
- **Low prices invite hesitation and skepticism** — premium pricing creates confidence.
- **You do not need to "prove" yourself with low prices** — your results speak for themselves.
- **High-value pricing attracts high-value clients** who respect your time and expertise.
- **When you confidently charge more**, you position yourself as a leader in your industry.

Pricing is not just about money — it is about positioning, perception, and attracting the right people.

The moment you own your value, set premium prices, and confidently communicate them, you will:

- Work with better clients.
- Make more money with less effort.
- Have more freedom and energy to grow your business.
- Step into the wealth and success you truly deserve.

It is time to stop justifying your prices and start owning them.

You are not just offering a service — you are offering a premium transformation. Charge accordingly.

How to Position Yourself as A Premium Brand

Pricing is not just about numbers — it's about positioning, perception, and the experience you create.

A premium brand does not compete on price. It commands attention, trust, and high-value clients who are ready to invest.

If you want to charge premium prices, you must position yourself as a high-value expert — not just another service provider.

Premium pricing is not about being expensive for the sake of it. It is about aligning your price with the value, transformation, and exclusivity you offer.

Here's how to elevate your brand and attract clients who are happy to pay what you're worth.

Step 1: Stop Competing on Price — Compete on Value

One of the biggest mistakes women make is trying to be "affordable" instead of being irreplaceable.

- Low-cost brands compete on price.
- Premium brands compete on transformation, authority, and exclusivity.

High-value clients do not search for the cheapest option — they search for the best.

Instead of asking, "*How can I be more affordable?*" ask, "*How can I be the only choice for my ideal client?*"

Step 2: Build Authority and Trust

Premium brands do not chase clients — clients come to them.

The key to this? Authority and trust.

Ways to establish yourself as an expert in your field:

- Content marketing — Share valuable insights through blogs, YouTube, podcasts, or social media.
- Speaking engagements and interviews — Position yourself as a thought leader in your industry.
- Client results and testimonials — Showcase success stories and transformations.
- Consistent messaging — Speak with confidence and certainty in everything you do.

High-value clients invest in experts. If you position yourself as the authority, price resistance disappears.

Step 3: Upgrade Your Brand Presence

People make snap judgments about value and quality based on visual branding, messaging, and overall experience.

- Professional and polished website — Your website should communicate exclusivity, clarity, and confidence.
- Luxury-feel branding — Colors, fonts, and visuals should align with a premium experience.

- Consistent high-value messaging — Your words should feel empowered, direct, and confident.
- Exclusive, not generic — Position yourself as the go-to person in your field, not just another option.

High-value clients expect a premium experience before they even pay you. Make your brand reflect that.

Step 4: Create an Elevated Client Experience

People do not just pay for what you do — they pay for how you do it.

Premium brands deliver flawless, seamless, high-end client experiences that make people feel valued and confident in their investment.

- Simplified, streamlined onboarding — Make it effortless for clients to buy from you.
- Exclusive access and high-touch support — Create a VIP experience for premium offers.
- Clear boundaries and professionalism — Premium brands do not over-serve or undercharge.
- Quality over quantity — Focus on serving a select group of high-caliber clients instead of trying to appeal to everyone.

Luxury brands are never chaotic or unclear — build a brand that reflects clarity, ease, and professionalism.

Step 5: Package Your Offers Like a High-Value Experience

A premium brand does not just offer services — it offers solutions and transformations.

How to structure your offers for premium positioning:

- Offer tiers of service: Have a high-end option (VIP, private consulting) alongside mid-range scalable offers (courses, memberships).
- Focus on results, not just process: Sell the outcome, not just the steps.
- Use premium language: Stop saying "buy my program" — start saying "apply to work with me."
- Communicate exclusivity: Create application-only programs or limited-availability offers.

Premium clients do not buy "sessions" or "hours" — they invest in transformation and results.

Step 6: Own Your Prices with Confidence

Your energy around pricing will dictate whether people accept or reject your offers.

- State your prices with certainty — No hesitation, no apologies, no justifications.
- Be firm on your rates — Never lower your prices for someone who cannot afford you.
- Position high prices as normal — Frame your investment as the industry standard, not something unusual.
- Eliminate discount culture — Premium brands never discount their services.

Your confidence in your pricing teaches people how to perceive your value.

Step 7: Create Demand Through Exclusivity

People want what feels rare, valuable, and exclusive.

To increase perceived value:

- Limit availability: Create high-end offers that are available for select clients only.
- Raise prices over time: Show that your demand is growing.

- Control access: Make certain offers application-only.
- Deliver beyond expectations: Make every client experience feel like a premium investment.

Exclusivity increases demand. The less available you are, the more valuable you become.

The *Fast-Track Millionairess* Premium Brand Formula

- **Stop competing on price** — position yourself as the only choice in your field.
- **Build authority through** content, testimonials, and public visibility.
- **Upgrade your brand presence** — your visuals and messaging must reflect exclusivity.
- **Create a flawless, high-end client experience** that justifies premium pricing.
- **Package your offers** as transformational, not transactional.
- **Own your prices with confidence** — people pay for certainty.
- **Increase demand through exclusivity** — high-value clients seek out rare, premium opportunities.

People do not invest in what is common — they invest in what feels premium, exclusive, and high-impact.

The moment you stop positioning yourself as "affordable" and start presenting yourself as an industry leader, everything shifts.

- Better clients
- Higher income
- Less resistance to pricing
- More impact with less effort

You are not just selling a service — you are offering a high-value, life-changing experience. Price and position yourself accordingly.

Chapter 8: Financial Confidence — Mastering Money as a Millionairess

Shifting from Scarcity Thinking to Wealth Mindset

Most women want financial freedom. They want abundance, success, and a life of wealth.

But instead of engaging with money, learning about it, and taking ownership of their financial future, they default to wishful thinking.

Women have been sold the idea that they can "manifest" wealth by closing their eyes, visualizing money, and waiting for it to arrive.

This is bullshit.

Manifestation does not work if you refuse to engage with the very thing you are trying to attract.

You do not manifest by wishing — you manifest by mastering.

If you want to be a millionairess, you need to:

- Open your eyes and get close to your finances.
- Understand how money works, moves, and grows.
- Stop avoiding numbers, stop making excuses, and start taking full control.

A business without cash flow is not a business — it's a hobby that's waiting to fail.

If you avoid financial mastery, do not dare feel jealous of the women who succeed. The ones who make it are not "lucky" — they are engaged, informed, and in control.

Why Women Struggle with Financial Confidence

For too long, women have been discouraged from engaging with money. Society has conditioned them to:

- Believe money is "too complicated" or "not their strength."
- Hand financial control to men, accountants, or financial advisors.
- Think that engaging with money is "stressful" or "not feminine."
- Feel shame around charging, spending, or investing.
- Expect someone else (a boss, a husband, the universe) to provide for them.

This financial avoidance is a learned behavior — not an actual limitation.

And it has to stop.

No one is coming to rescue you financially. No one is going to build your wealth for you.

If you want financial power, you need to own it.

Breaking Free from the Scarcity Mindset

A scarcity mindset keeps women trapped in financial struggle. It makes them believe:

- I'm not good with money.
- Money is hard to make and even harder to keep.
- If I charge more, people won't pay.
- Wealth is for other people, not for me.
- I don't need to understand money; I just need to attract it.

This thinking guarantees financial failure.

To become a millionairess, you must shift into a wealth mindset — one that is based on action, responsibility, and financial engagement.

Fast-Track Millionairess

Your financial reality is a direct reflection of your financial mindset and habits.

Here's how to shift from scarcity thinking to financial power:

Stop Hoping — Start Learning

Money is not mystical, random, or difficult. It is a simple system of numbers, patterns, and decisions.

If you don't understand cash flow, profit margins, and financial strategy, your business will never scale.

If you avoid bank reconciliations, pricing structures, and financial forecasting, you are running your business blindfolded.

You do not attract wealth by avoiding numbers — you attract it by mastering them.

Take Radical Responsibility for Your Finances

- Know exactly how much money is coming in, going out, and growing.
- Create a cash flow forecast — predict your income and expenses so there are no surprises.
- Do your bank reconciliations weekly — stop avoiding your accounts.
- Track your financial growth strategy — how will you scale your revenue over the next 12 months?

Wealthy women do not "hope" their finances work out — they plan, track, and adjust with precision.

See Money as a Tool, Not an Emotion

Money is not good or bad — it is neutral. It is a tool that expands opportunities.

Stop making money emotional — it is not a reflection of your worth. It is simply a measure of value creation and financial strategy.

If money triggers you, get curious about why — what beliefs have you inherited that are keeping you stuck?

Detach from fear, guilt, or shame around money. The more neutral and empowered you are, the more you will attract and retain wealth.

Price for Profit, Not Just Survival

If your business is barely covering expenses, you are pricing too low.

Your prices must cover: Business costs, taxes and financial obligations and your personal wealth-building strategy

Stop charging what feels safe and start charging what fuels financial growth.

Businesses that thrive are priced for profit — not for survival.

Master Cash Flow Like a Millionairess

Cash flow is more important than revenue.

A million-dollar business with bad cash flow can go bankrupt.

To master cash flow:

- Track all income and expenses daily.
- Forecast future revenue and costs.
- Set aside money for taxes, investments, and scaling.
- Pay yourself first — do not run a business that cannot sustain you.

If you are not in control of your cash flow, you are not in control of your business.

Invest — Don't Just Earn

Earning money is step one — but wealth is built through smart investing.

Fast-Track Millionairess

Put your money to work in stocks, real estate, business investments, and assets that grow over time.

Stop hoarding money out of fear — let it circulate in ways that generate more wealth.

Millionaires do not just make money — they multiply it.

Cut Off Financial Excuses Immediately

I'm not good with numbers → Then learn.

I don't have time to track my finances → Then you don't have time to be wealthy.

Money is stressful → Only when you ignore it.

I just want to help people — I'm not doing this for the money → Then you won't be able to sustain your impact.

If you do not take control of your money, someone else will — and they will not have your best interests at heart.

The Fast-Track Millionairess Financial Formula

- **Money is not something to fear** — it is something to master.
- **You do not manifest wealth by wishing** — you manifest it by engaging.
- **Financial success requires** daily tracking, planning, and forecasting.
- **Businesses without financial mastery fail** — it is not optional.
- **You have no right to be jealous of wealthy women** if you refuse to learn about money.
- **The most powerful women are the ones who know** exactly where their money is, how it works, and where it's going next.

Wealth does not come to those who wait — it comes to those who take full financial control.

Fast-Track Millionairess

If you are serious about becoming a millionairess, then stop waiting, stop avoiding, and stop making excuses.

Your financial future is in your hands.

Roll up your sleeves, take ownership, and start acting like the wealthy woman you were meant to be.

Smart Investing for Long-Term Freedom

Most women focus only on earning money — but the real secret to financial freedom is learning how to grow and multiply wealth.

Wealth is not just about what you make — it's about what you keep and how you make that money work for you.

Many women stay stuck in financial stress because they do not:

- Pay down debt fast enough
- Understand how to build assets
- Invest their money wisely

If you want true long-term financial freedom, you must stop relying solely on income and start creating wealth through smart financial strategies.

Earning makes you comfortable. Investing makes you rich.

Step 1: Pay Down Debt as Quickly as Possible

Before you focus on building investments, you must eliminate toxic financial burdens.

Debt is the single biggest drain on wealth.

Every month you carry debt, you are paying interest instead of building assets.

Fast-Track Millionairess

High-interest debt keeps you financially stuck, no matter how much you earn.

If you do not aggressively pay down debt, you are delaying your financial freedom.

You cannot build wealth while leaking money through unnecessary debt payments.

How to Pay Off Debt Faster:

- Stop making minimum payments — increase your payments aggressively.
- Use the snowball method (pay off the smallest debt first, then roll payments into the next).
- Refinance or negotiate interest rates — reduce how much money is going to the bank instead of you.
- Cut unnecessary expenses and redirect that money toward debt.

Every pound you throw at debt today is a pound you can invest tomorrow.

Once your high-interest debts are eliminated, your money is yours to grow.

Step 2: Build an Emergency Fund (So You Never Depend on Debt Again)

Before investing, you need a financial safety net.

A strong emergency fund prevents you from falling back into debt when unexpected expenses arise.

Goal: Save 3–6 months' worth of living expenses.

Keep this money separate — it is not for spending, investing, or business growth.

Use a high-yield savings account so your money earns interest while sitting.

This fund is not for luxury spending — it is for peace of mind and financial resilience.

Fast-Track Millionairess

Once your debt is gone and your emergency fund is set, you are ready to build true wealth.

Step 3: Start Investing — Let Your Money Work for You

Wealthy women do not just make money — they make their money work for them.

If your money is just sitting in a bank account, you are losing money to inflation.

Investing is not optional if you want financial freedom — it is how you build lasting wealth.

Where to Invest for Long-Term Wealth Growth:

- Stock Market — Long-term investing in stocks and index funds generates compounded wealth growth.
- Real Estate — Property investments create passive income and long-term value appreciation.
- Business Investments — Starting or investing in businesses can create exponential financial returns.
- Dividend Stocks — Certain stocks pay passive income regularly, creating extra cash flow.
- Retirement Accounts and Pensions — Maximizing tax-free investment growth is crucial for financial security.

Investing is not gambling — it is strategically growing your money over time.

Step 4: Focus on Passive Income Investments

To create true financial freedom, you need income that flows in without you working for it.

Passive income means your money works for you, even when you sleep.

Some of the best passive investment strategies include:

- Dividend Stocks — Invest in companies that pay regular profit distributions.
- Rental Properties — Earn income from tenants while your property value increases.
- Index Funds and ETFs — Automated stock market investments that grow over time.
- High-Yield Savings and Bonds — Safe, steady returns on your money.

The goal is to build multiple income streams that generate wealth without trading time for money.

Step 5: Automate Your Wealth Growth

Once your money is working for you, make sure it continues growing automatically.

Set up automatic transfers into investment accounts — treat investing like a non-negotiable bill.

Use compound interest to your advantage — reinvest your earnings instead of spending them.

Avoid impulsive financial decisions — wealth is built through long-term consistency, not quick wins.

Financial freedom is not about one-time success — it's about creating an automated system that keeps working for you forever.

Step 6: Think Like a Millionairess — Not Like a Spender

Rich people do not think about what they can "buy" with their money.

They think about:

- How their money can make them more money.

- How they can protect and multiply their assets.
- How to reinvest profits instead of spending them.

Wealthy women do not just increase their income — they increase their ownership, assets, and investments.

The *Fast-Track Millionairess* Investment Formula

- **Pay down debt fast** — do not let interest drain your future wealth.
- **Build an emergency fund** — so you never rely on debt again.
- **Start investing** — your money must work for you, not just sit in a bank.
- **Focus on passive income** — so you are not always trading time for money.
- **Automate wealth growth** — set up financial systems that grow your money automatically.
- **Think like an investor** — wealthy women focus on assets, not just spending.

Wealth is not created by saving — it is created by multiplying what you have.

You will never reach millionairess status by simply working harder, saving a little, and hoping for the best.

You reach it by mastering your money, eliminating debt, and investing strategically.

The moment you stop avoiding money and start commanding it, your financial reality will change forever.

How to Create Financial Safety Nets While Scaling Up

Scaling a business and growing wealth requires financial risk — but it should be calculated, not reckless.

Too many women jump into expansion without safety nets, leaving themselves vulnerable to cash flow crises, unexpected downturns, and financial stress.

Fast-Track Millionairess

True financial freedom is not just about making more money — it is about protecting yourself as you grow.

The goal is to scale up while maintaining financial stability, so no setback can wipe you out.

Here's how to create financial safety nets while expanding your income and investments.

Step 1: Build a "No-Stress" Emergency Fund

An emergency fund is your first financial safety net. It ensures you never have to rely on loans, credit cards, or desperate business moves when things get tough.

- Personal Emergency Fund — 3–6 months of living expenses saved in a separate account.
- Business Emergency Fund — Enough to cover 3–6 months of business operating costs.

This buffer protects you from unexpected downturns while giving you the confidence to scale up.

Step 2: Always Maintain Positive Cash Flow

Many businesses fail not because they aren't profitable, but because they run out of cash.

To avoid this:

- Track your cash flow at least weekly, if not daily — Know exactly how much money is coming in and going out.
- Never spend future money before it arrives — Operate based on what's in your account now, not what you expect to come in.
- Have a cash reserve for unexpected business expenses — A large invoice, tax bill, or supplier delay should not throw you into panic mode.

Scaling a business should never put you in a cash crisis — always keep a buffer.

Step 3: Pay Yourself First (Even When Scaling Up)

Many entrepreneurs put every dollar back into their business, leaving themselves financially unstable.

This is dangerous because:

- If your business has a slow month, you personally suffer.
- You are not building personal wealth outside of your business.
- It creates a cycle where you are trapped in "reinvesting" without personal financial security.

Always take a sensible percentage of your revenue as personal income.

Allocate money to personal investments, savings, and wealth-building — NOT just back into business expenses.

Treat yourself like an employee — your financial well-being matters.

A business that scales should support your lifestyle, not leave you financially unstable.

Step 4: Diversify Your Income Streams

If you rely on one income source, you are financially vulnerable.

Even if you are making great money right now, a single stream of income is risky.

- Create multiple revenue streams within your business — (e.g., coaching, courses, digital products, affiliate income).
- Invest in assets outside of your business — (stocks, real estate, passive income investments).
- Ensure your money is working in different places — so one setback does not wipe you out.

The wealthiest women do not rely on just one source of income — they have multiple streams flowing at all times.

Step 5: Scale Smart — Not Desperately

Many entrepreneurs expand too quickly, taking on:

- Too many overhead expenses
- Expensive hires before they're needed
- Debt-fueled growth that puts them at risk

Scale in stages, not in desperation.

- Keep overheads lean — only increase costs when absolutely necessary.
- Use profits to scale, not debt — invest from surplus, not loans.
- Test new offers before making massive commitments — grow based on demand, not wishful thinking.

Fast growth is meaningless if it's unstable — always scale in a way that protects your finances.

Step 6: Insure and Legally Protect Yourself

No one likes to think about financial disasters, lawsuits, or unexpected events, but ignoring them can destroy everything you've built.

- Have solid business contracts — Protect yourself from non-paying clients, disputes, or legal risks.
- Get business insurance — So one bad client or mistake does not cost you everything.
- Separate personal and business finances — Your personal assets should never be at risk from business liabilities.
- Protect your intellectual property — If your ideas, content, or work are valuable, ensure they are legally protected.

Fast-Track Millionairess

Smart women do not wait for financial disasters — they prevent them before they happen.

Step 7: Set Up an Automated Wealth System

Once your business is making consistent money, ensure that your wealth continues growing automatically.

- Automate investments — Have money flow into stocks, retirement accounts, or real estate without you thinking about it.
- Automate savings — Set up transfers to a financial buffer or long-term wealth accounts.
- Create a financial freedom plan — Know exactly what your money is doing for you in 5, 10, and 20 years.

The goal is not just short-term income — it is building a financial system that keeps you wealthy for life.

The *Fast-Track Millionairess* Safety Net Formula

- **Always have an emergency fund** — never operate without a financial cushion.
- **Maintain positive cash flow** — running out of money kills businesses faster than anything else.
- **Pay yourself first** — your business should build YOUR wealth, not just itself.
- **Diversify your income** — never rely on just one stream of money.
- **Scale wisely** — growth should never create financial instability.
- **Protect yourself legally and financially** — do not leave yourself open to risk.
- **Automate your wealth** — your money should be growing in the background at all times.

Scaling should feel exciting, not stressful — if you are constantly worried about money, you are doing it wrong.

The goal is to build wealth and success, while always having financial security behind you.

A millionairess is not just rich — she is financially untouchable.

Developing A Millionaire-Level Relationship with Money

Most people treat money as something external — a thing they need, chase, or stress over.

Millionairesses treat money as an intimate, trusted partner — something they command, respect, and actively build a relationship with.

Your relationship with money determines your financial reality. If you see money as difficult, scarce, or intimidating, it will always feel out of reach. If you see it as a tool, a game, and a resource to master, it will always flow to you.

Signs of a Weak Relationship with Money

If money feels like:

- Something you avoid or feel anxious about
- A topic you don't want to engage with
- Something you think about only when you "need" it
- A constant source of stress or uncertainty
- A thing other people have, but not you

Then your relationship with money needs serious rewiring.

A millionairess does not just "make" money — she builds a deep, powerful connection with it.

Fast-Track Millionairess

Stop Seeing Money as Emotional — Start Seeing It as a Tool

Many women tie money to guilt, shame, or self-worth.

- They feel guilty for charging more.
- They feel ashamed for wanting financial success.
- They assume making money means taking from others.

Money is neutral. It is neither good nor bad. It is simply a tool — a resource that expands your ability to create, help, and grow.

Instead of asking: *Do I deserve this money?*

Ask: *How can I manage and multiply this resource to create the life I want?*

Engage with Money Daily (Stop Avoiding It!)

Many women only look at their finances when things are going wrong.

Millionairesses engage with their money every single day.

- Check your bank accounts daily — know exactly what's coming in and going out.
- Track cash flow weekly — set a time to look at all business and personal finances.
- Plan your money goals monthly — where is your money growing, investing, and working for you?

Ignoring money creates financial chaos. The more time you spend mastering it, the more money flows to you.

Shift from Scarcity to Ownership

A scarcity mindset says:

- *I hope I make enough.*

- Money is hard to come by.
- I shouldn't charge too much.

A millionaire mindset says:

- I create my own financial reality.
- Money is limitless when I manage it well.
- I charge for the real value I provide.

You do not "hope" for money or "manifest" without a clear action plan — you command and create it.

Pay Yourself First — Always

Millionairesses never leave themselves for last financially.

- Before paying bills, employees, or reinvesting, they pay themselves first.
- They allocate money for savings, investments, and personal wealth-building first — THEN they handle business expenses.
- They do not overwork and underpay themselves in their own business.

If you don't pay yourself first, you are running a business that only benefits others, not you.

Speak About Money with Power

Language shapes reality.

Weak money language:

- I can't afford that.
- I'm just not good with money.
- Money is stressful.

Fast-Track Millionairess

Millionairess money language:

- *How can I create the money for this?*
- *I am in control of my financial success.*
- *Money flows easily to me because I manage it wisely.*

Your words influence your actions — speak like someone who commands wealth.

Make Decisions Like a Wealthy Woman

Millionairesses do not delay financial decisions out of fear.

- They invest in themselves — they don't stay stuck in "*I can't afford it*" thinking.
- They do not wait for "*the right moment*" to learn money — they engage NOW.
- They think long-term — they do not make financial choices based on short-term emotions.

If you are waiting for permission to act wealthy, you will wait forever.

Master Financial Growth

Track your net worth — know exactly where your assets and liabilities stand.
Set clear financial goals — have targets for revenue, investments, and wealth.
Understand money growth strategies — stocks, real estate, passive income.
Invest instead of just saving — your money must work, not sit.

Wealth is not luck — it is structured financial mastery.

The *Fast-Track Millionairess* Money Formula

- **Your relationship with money** determines how much flows to you.
- **Engage with money daily** — treat it like a trusted partner, not a distant problem.
- **Stop seeing money as emotional** — it is a tool that you command.

Fast-Track Millionairess

- **Pay yourself first** — your wealth comes before business expenses.
- **Speak about money with power** — your language shapes your financial future.
- **Think, act, and invest like a wealthy woman** — because you are one.

You do not "become" a millionairess — you start acting like one now, and the money follows.

PART THREE: EMBODYING YOUR MILLIONAIRESS IDENTITY

Stepping into the Power of Wealth and Leadership

Chapter 9: Unapologetic Wealth — Owning Your Success Without Guilt

Breaking Free from the "Good Girl" Conditioning

Women have been conditioned to believe that being "good" means being small, quiet, self-sacrificing, and humble.

- Good girls do not take up space.
- Good girls do not talk about money.
- Good girls do not ask for too much.
- Good girls are grateful for what they get, even if it is less than they deserve.

This conditioning is a wealth killer. It keeps women undercharging, over-apologizing, and waiting for permission to succeed.

If you want to become a millionairess, you must break free from the "good girl" identity and step into unapologetic ownership of your success.

How "Good Girl" Conditioning Sabotages Wealth

From a young age, women are taught that their role is to:

- Be agreeable, not assertive. Which makes them hesitate in negotiations.
- Be liked, not intimidating. Which makes them lower their prices.
- Be supportive, not the leader. Which makes them stay in the background.
- Be grateful, not demanding. Which makes them accept less than they're worth.
- Be generous, not transactional. Which makes them over-give and undercharge.

The result? Women end up working twice as hard for half as much, afraid that being too bold, too wealthy, or too ambitious will make them "unlikable."

Give Yourself Permission to Want More

- Women have been conditioned to feel guilty for wanting wealth.
- Many believe success comes at the cost of kindness, love, or femininity.
- Some fear that earning more will make them less relatable or less accepted.

Here's the truth: There is NOTHING wrong with wanting wealth. Money does not change who you are — it amplifies it. If you are kind, generous, and powerful now, money will only expand that.

Instead of thinking, Who am I to want more? ask:

- Who am I NOT to step into my highest potential?
- What impact can I make when I allow myself to thrive?
- Why should I be anything less than my full, abundant self?

Stop Shrinking Yourself to Make Others Comfortable

Many women **downplay their success** so they do not intimidate others.

- They hide their wins so they don't seem "braggy."
- They avoid talking about money because it might make someone uncomfortable.
- They downplay their financial goals to seem "humble."

Stop minimizing yourself to fit inside someone else's comfort zone.

Your success does not take away from anyone else.
Playing small does not serve you — or the people who need your leadership.
You are not responsible for how others feel about your ambition.

A millionairess does not shrink to fit — she expands and invites others to rise with her.

Fast-Track Millionairess

Stop Seeking Approval — Own Your Decisions

Many women hesitate to step into wealth because they fear judgment.

- What will my family think if I start making more than them?
- What if my friends judge me for my ambition?
- What if people think I'm selfish, greedy, or materialistic?

Here's the reality:

- People will judge you no matter what you do. Whether you are struggling or thriving, someone will have an opinion.
- You do not need permission to be successful. No one else gets to decide how big you are allowed to become.
- You will never be truly free until you stop seeking external validation.

A millionairess does not wait for approval — she builds her own empire and lets the world adjust.

Stop Apologizing for Charging, Earning, and Thriving

Women are often taught to feel bad about money.

They apologize for their prices.
They feel guilty about earning more than their partners, peers, or family.
They hesitate to talk about wealth because they don't want to seem arrogant.

Stop apologizing for what you deserve. Your wealth is NOT something to be ashamed of — it is something to be celebrated.

A millionairess does not ask for permission to charge her worth — she expects it.

Be Unapologetically Bold About Your Success

You do not need to:

- Water yourself down to be accepted.
- Pretend you don't care about wealth to seem "humble."
- Stay small so others do not feel uncomfortable.

Instead:

- Own your ambition, without hesitation.
- Talk about wealth, money, and success without shame.
- Be proud of your financial achievements — and let them inspire others.

Your success is not just about you — it is about showing other women what is possible.

A millionairess does not shrink. She leads, she earns, and she thrives — unapologetically.

The *Fast-Track Millionairess* Success Formula

- **You do not need permission to want more** — your ambition is valid.
- **Playing small does not serve you or the world** — step into your full power.
- **Approval-seeking will keep you broke** — own your success, unapologetically.
- **Wealth is not shameful** — it is an expansion of your highest potential.
- **A millionairess does not ask for permission to thrive** — she just does.

You are not here to play small. You are here to build, lead, and create impact. Own it fully.

Why Women Fear Outshining Others and How to Rise Anyway

Women are often taught to dim their own light so others don't feel uncomfortable.

They fear that if they become too successful, too wealthy, or too powerful, they will:

- Lose friendships.
- Be judged by family.
- Make others feel "less than."
- Be seen as arrogant, greedy, or unrelatable.

This is one of the biggest subconscious blocks to wealth — women fear that stepping into their full power will create rejection, jealousy, or resentment.

But here's the truth:

You cannot shrink yourself to protect other people's insecurities.

If your success triggers someone, that is their work to do — not yours.

Why Women Fear Outshining Others

This fear comes from deep-rooted social conditioning that tells women:

- *Don't get too big, or people won't like you.* **False**.
- *Success makes women intimidating, and men won't want them.* **False**.
- *If you outgrow your friends, you'll be alone.* **False** — although you will find out who you real friends are.
- *Money changes people.* **False** — it reveals who they already are.

None of this is true. But if you believe it, you will keep playing small to "stay safe."

The reality is:

- True friends celebrate your growth, not resent it.
- Your wealth does not take from others — it expands possibilities.
- The right people will rise with you, not hold you back.

Reframe Success as an Invitation, Not a Threat

Your success does not make others small — it shows them what is possible.

If someone feels "less than" because of your success, it is a reflection of their own self-worth, not your actions.

The best way to uplift others is to lead by example, not shrink to make them comfortable.

You can either inspire people or make them comfortable. You do not owe anyone smallness.

Let Go of People Who Can't Celebrate You

If your success makes someone resentful, that is a sign they were never truly rooting for you.

If they need you to stay small to feel good about themselves, that is not friendship — it is control.

A millionairess does not keep people in her life who punish her for thriving.

Instead, surround yourself with:

- Women (and men) who are also rising.
- Mentors who challenge you to go bigger.
- People who genuinely celebrate your wins.

Your circle should expand with your success, not contract because of it.

Stop Feeling Guilty for Winning

Many women feel guilt when they:

- Start making more money than their friends or family.
- Gain recognition while others struggle.
- Have opportunities that others don't.

Guilt will keep you broke. You do not have to apologize for what you have worked for.

Instead of shrinking, use your wealth and success to:

- Create jobs.
- Support causes you care about.
- Teach and uplift others.
- Be an example of what's possible.

A millionairess does not feel bad for thriving — she leverages her success to create more good in the world.

Own That Some People Will Be Jealous — And That's OK

- Not everyone will celebrate you.
- Some people will feel triggered.
- Some will project their insecurities onto you.
- And that is not your problem.
- You are not responsible for how others feel about your success.

Instead of dimming your light, remind yourself:

- You did the work to get here.
- You are worthy of your success.
- You are allowed to thrive without shame.

If people judge you for rising, let them watch. But do not let them stop you.

Give Yourself Full Permission to Be Big

If you keep yourself small, you are not just holding yourself back — you are holding back every woman who needs to see what's possible.

You playing small serves no one. But you playing big changes everything.

Fast-Track Millionairess

A millionairess does not fear her own power — she owns it fully, without apology.

The *Fast-Track Millionairess* Success Formula

- **You do not need to shrink** to make others comfortable.
- **Your success is not selfish** — it is an invitation for others to rise.
- **If people cannot celebrate you**, they are not your people.
- **Guilt will keep you broke** — own your wealth unapologetically.
- **Not everyone will be happy for you**, and that's OK — rise anyway.

You are here to thrive, not to stay small. Give yourself permission to take up space, create wealth, and own your success — without guilt, without fear, and without apology.

Handling Criticism and Judgment from Family, Friends, and Society

Stepping into wealth, success, and power will trigger people.

Not everyone will celebrate you. Some will:

- Criticize you for charging more.
- Judge you for wanting wealth.
- Question your ambition.
- Try to pull you back into "reality."

This is not a sign to stop — it is confirmation that you are breaking the mold.

Why People Criticize Successful Women

Criticism does not come from people who are thriving — it comes from those who feel left behind, threatened, or uncomfortable with your rise.

- Family may feel insecure — If you start earning more than them, they may feel like they are "falling behind."

- Friends may feel left out — If your success changes your lifestyle, they may worry they will no longer relate to you.
- Society is conditioned to distrust wealthy women — Powerful women are still judged more harshly than powerful men.

People project their fears, limitations, and insecurities onto those who rise. That has nothing to do with you.

Stop Taking Criticism Personally

If someone judges your success, it is about them — not you.

- Their comments reveal their fears about money, success, and self-worth.
- Their discomfort comes from their own beliefs about what's possible for them.
- Their judgment is a reflection of where they feel stuck — not a reflection of your actions.

The moment you stop internalizing other people's opinions, you become unstoppable.

Set Boundaries with Negative People

If someone consistently criticizes your ambition, wealth, or success, they are not supporting you.

Instead of:

- Defending yourself
- Trying to change their mind
- Watering yourself down to please them

Do this instead:

- Set clear boundaries — You do not have to justify your success to anyone.

- Limit your exposure — Reduce time with people who drain your energy.
- Surround yourself with people who uplift you — Expand your circle to include other ambitious women.

You are not responsible for making other people comfortable with your success.

A millionairess does not explain, argue, or prove herself — she simply moves forward.

Stay Focused on Your Vision

People will have opinions — but opinions don't build empires.

Every moment you spend defending yourself to critics is a moment you could be using to grow, create, and build.

- Stop asking for approval from people who do not have the results you want.
- Do not waste energy explaining your vision to those who refuse to see it.
- Your purpose is not to convince — it is to lead.

Stay focused on your future, not on people who are stuck in their past.

Own Your Success Without Guilt or Apology

Many women feel the need to "soften" their success to make others comfortable.

- They downplay their wins.
- They pretend money doesn't matter.
- They hide their ambition to avoid judgment.

Stop making yourself small to protect other people's feelings.

You are allowed to be proud of your success, your wealth, and your power. Own it fully.

Turn Criticism into Fuel

Instead of shrinking in response to judgment, let it push you forward.

- Prove to yourself that you can rise, no matter who doubts you.
- Use their words as motivation to keep going.
- Let your success be the loudest response.

Your success will either inspire people or expose their insecurities. Either way, it is not your job to fix them.

A millionairess does not fear judgment — she expects it and rises anyway.

The *Fast-Track Millionairess* Success Formula

- **Criticism does not come from people ahead of you** — it comes from those who feel left behind.
- **Other people's insecurities** are not your responsibility.
- **You do not owe anyone** an explanation for your ambition.
- **Set boundaries** — your energy is too valuable to waste on negativity.
- **The best response to judgment is success** — keep rising.

You were not meant to stay small. You were meant to rise, lead, and create wealth — without fear, without apology, and without limits.

Creating Boundaries and Walking Away from Unhealthy Situations

One of the biggest differences between women who rise into wealth and success and those who stay stuck is boundaries.

Millionairesses do not tolerate energy leaks, toxic relationships, or unaligned commitments. They protect their time, money, and emotional energy with absolute clarity.

Fast-Track Millionairess

If you are going to build a life of freedom, wealth, and power, you must stop allowing unhealthy situations to drain you.

This means walking away from:

- People who undermine, manipulate, hold you back, or devalue you.
- Business situations that exhaust you but do not serve your future.
- Clients who disrespect your time, energy, or worth.
- Conversations that lower your confidence or energy.

A millionairess does not argue, beg, or explain herself — she sets the boundary and moves on.

Recognize What Is Draining You

If something feels heavy, draining, or misaligned, it is costing you more than you realize.

Ask yourself:

- Who or what is taking more than they give?
- What situations make you feel undervalued, disrespected, or exhausted?
- Where are you tolerating things out of obligation or guilt?

Your energy is your most valuable asset — anything that drains it is blocking your next level of success.

If it costs you your peace, it is too expensive.

Decide What You Will No Longer Tolerate

People will treat you based on what you allow.

If you undercharge, overgive, and accept disrespect, people will keep taking.

- Stop allowing toxic relationships to continue just because they are familiar.

- Stop saying yes to things that drain you.
- Stop keeping people in your life out of guilt.

What you tolerate today becomes your standard tomorrow. Raise your standards.

A millionairess sets her terms — and she does not negotiate them.

Communicate Boundaries Clearly — Without Guilt

- You do not need to justify or over-explain.
- You do not need to apologize for protecting your energy.
- You do not need to "be nice" at the expense of your well-being.

A boundary is not an invitation for negotiation — it is a statement of self-respect.

Examples of Strong Boundaries:

- *"I do not work with clients who expect discounts or do not respect my time."*
- *"I do not engage in conversations that lower my energy or confidence."*
- *"I am no longer available for relationships that do not feel aligned."*

A millionairess does not ask for permission to protect herself — she simply does it.

Walk Away When Necessary

Some situations cannot be fixed — they must be left behind.

- If a business partnership is toxic — leave it.
- If a client drains you — fire them.
- If a friendship no longer serves you — let it go.
- If a conversation is disrespectful — end it.

Not everyone gets lifetime access to you. Some chapters must close for the next one to begin.

Fast-Track Millionairess

A millionairess does not cling to what is misaligned — she releases it and moves forward.

Stop Feeling Responsible for Other People's Reactions

When you set boundaries, some people will react badly. That is their issue, not yours.

- People who benefit from your lack of boundaries will resist when you create them.
- People who truly respect you will accept them without drama.

Your job is not to manage other people's emotions — it is to protect your energy.

Let people be upset. Let them adjust. But do not lower your boundaries to make them comfortable.

A millionairess does not make herself small to keep others happy.

Build a Life That Reflects Your Highest Standards

- Only work with people who respect your time and energy.
- Only surround yourself with people who uplift and empower you.
- Only commit to things that align with your vision and values.
- Only say yes when it is a full-body YES — never out of guilt or fear.

Boundaries are not about control — they are about creating a life that feels aligned, empowering, and abundant.

A millionairess is not available for anything that drains her, diminishes her, or disrespects her.

The Fast-Track Millionairess Boundaries Formula

- **Your energy is your most valuable asset** — protect it fiercely.
- **You do not owe anyone** unlimited access to you.

Fast-Track Millionairess

- **Tolerating the wrong people and situations** costs you success.
- **Saying NO to what drains you** creates space for what uplifts you.
- **The right people will respect your boundaries** — the wrong ones will resist them.
- **You do not need permission to walk away** from what no longer serves you.

You are not here to be drained, overworked, or undervalued. You are here to thrive, lead, and build an empire on your terms.

Set the boundary. Enforce the boundary. And never feel guilty for protecting your peace.

Chapter 10: Feminine Power in a Masculine Energy World — Leading with Impact

The Art of Intuitive Decision-Making in Business

In a world where logic, structure, and strategy are praised as the ultimate tools for success, women's natural intuitive power has been undervalued.

The most powerful and successful women are not just strategic — they are deeply intuitive.

- They do not follow rigid rules — they trust their instincts.
- They do not wait for external validation — they listen to their inner knowing.
- They do not just make decisions with their mind — they make them with their whole being.

Millionairesses blend logic with intuition, creating a business that is both strategic and soul-led.

Why Women's Intuition is a Business Superpower

Masculine energy is linear, structured, and numbers-driven. It wants to see facts, projections, and spreadsheets before making a move.

Feminine energy is fluid, creative, and instinctual. It senses timing, alignment, and energetic shifts before something becomes visible.

Women are wired for intuitive intelligence. But most ignore it because they've been told:

- *If it isn't logical, it isn't valid.*
- *You need more proof before you take action.*
- *If you can't explain why, it must not be right.*

Business success is not just about making the "right" decisions — it is about making aligned decisions at the right time.

A millionairess does not second-guess her intuition — she sharpens it and completely trusts it.

Recognize How Intuition Speaks to You

Your intuition is always communicating. It shows up as:

- A gut feeling — Instant knowing, even when logic says otherwise.
- Energy shifts — Something "feels off" or "feels right" without explanation.
- Body signals — Tension, ease, excitement, or resistance in your body.
- Synchronicities — Repeating signs, patterns, or messages guiding you.

Your intuition speaks in quiet nudges, not loud commands. The more you listen, the stronger it becomes.

A millionairess does not ignore her body's wisdom — she uses it as a decision-making tool.

Balance Intuition with Strategy

Ignoring intuition leads to burnout, frustration, and missed opportunities. Ignoring logic leads to chaos, instability, and poor execution.

The sweet spot is integrating both.

Before making a decision, ask yourself:

- LOGIC: *Does this make sense practically?*
- INTUITION: *Does this feel aligned, expansive, and right for me?*

If logic says YES but intuition says NO → Don't do it.

If intuition says YES but logic says NO → Get creative and find a way.

If both say YES → Move forward with full confidence.

A millionairess does not choose between intuition and logic — she uses both to lead with clarity.

Stop Asking for Permission — Trust Yourself First

Many women struggle with decision-making because they keep seeking external validation.

- *What do you think I should do?*
- *Does this sound like a good idea?*
- *Maybe I need more opinions before I decide.*

The more you ask others, the more disconnected you become from your own inner guidance.

A millionairess makes decisions from within — not from the opinions of people who are not living her vision.

Follow the Energy, Not Just the Plan

Business is not just about structured plans — it is about energetic timing.

- If an opportunity lights you up and aligns, act on it fast.
- If something drains you or feels forced, step back and reassess.
- If resistance keeps showing up, it is a sign to pivot — not push harder.

Your energy is your best business compass — listen to it more than external noise.

A millionairess does not push against resistance — she flows with alignment.

Make Decisions Quickly and Move with Certainty

Indecision kills success.

Fast-Track Millionairess

Overthinking is just fear disguised as logic.

The most successful women:

- Make decisions fast.
- Course-correct if needed.
- Do not waste time doubting themselves.

If you feel the pull to act, do it now. The longer you wait, the more fear creeps in.

A millionairess does not hesitate — she decides, she moves, and she trusts herself fully.

The *Fast-Track Millionairess* Decision-Making Formula

- **Your intuition is not a weakness** — it is a business advantage.
- **If it feels misaligned, do not force it**. If it feels right, move fast.
- **Stop asking for permission** — your inner knowing is more valuable than external opinions.
- **Follow the energy, not just the numbers.** Logic and strategy matter, but alignment wins.
- **Make decisions with speed and confidence** — indecision is the fastest way to kill momentum.

The most powerful women do not wait for certainty — they create it by trusting themselves.

A millionairess moves with clarity, certainty, and intuitive power — because she knows she is always guided.

Don't Allow Distorted Feminine or Distorted Masculine Energy to Put You Off Balance

In a world where success has traditionally been built on masculine principles, many women struggle to find their true leadership energy.

Fast-Track Millionairess

The secret to thriving as a millionairess is not rejecting masculine energy or overcompensating with forced femininity — it is learning to balance both.

True power comes from integrating the best of both energies while avoiding their distorted versions.

What is Balanced Masculine and Feminine Energy?

Balanced Masculine Energy is structured, strong, focused, and protective. Balanced Feminine Energy is creative, intuitive, receptive, and expansive.

When these energies are in harmony, they create:

- Confidence without arrogance
- Strength without aggression
- Wisdom without overthinking
- Success without burnout

The most powerful women know how to embody both energies as needed, creating wealth, impact, and fulfillment with ease.

The Dangers of Distorted Energy in Both Men and Women

Success and leadership require a balance of both masculine and feminine energy — but when either energy becomes distorted, it leads to dysfunction, burnout, and limitations.

Distorted Masculine Energy in Women

- Overworking, hustling, and forcing success through burnout
- Suppressing emotions and intuition to appear "strong"
- Becoming aggressive, defensive, or excessively competitive
- Believing that to win, they must outwork, outperform, or outfight everyone

Fast-Track Millionairess

This leads to exhaustion, resentment, and a loss of authentic power.

Distorted Feminine Energy in Women

- Waiting for success to "flow" without taking action
- Feeling helpless, lost, or lacking direction
- Giving away power in relationships, money, or business
- Resenting successful women instead of learning from them

This leads to stagnation, dependency, and unfulfilled potential.

Distorted Masculine Energy in Men

- Believing that domination and control are signs of strength
- Suppressing emotions to the point of emotional disconnection
- Seeking validation only through status, wealth, and external achievements
- Feeling threatened by successful women instead of seeing them as equals
- Viewing power as a competition instead of a responsibility

This leads to isolation, unfulfilling success, and a lack of true connection.

Distorted Feminine Energy in Men

- Lacking direction, drive, or a clear sense of purpose
- Being passive in decision-making and avoiding leadership
- Seeking external validation instead of developing internal confidence
- Resenting those who are successful instead of taking action toward growth
- Avoiding responsibility under the illusion of "just going with the flow"

This leads to frustration, stagnation, and a life that feels unfulfilled.

Fast-Track Millionairess

Why Integration is the Key to Success

Neither extreme leads to true wealth, leadership, or freedom.

Instead of rejecting or blaming masculine or feminine energy, we must learn to integrate both in a healthy, balanced way.

Masculine energy provides: Structure, action, strategy, focus, and protection. Feminine energy provides: Creativity, intuition, flow, emotional intelligence, and connection.

When these energies work together, we create powerful, sustainable success — one that is aligned, fulfilling, and impactful.

A millionairess is not stuck in distortion — she embodies the best of both energies, creating a business and life that thrives on balance, not burnout.

This creates true equality — not through blame or resentment, but through each person stepping into their full power, regardless of gender.

Balanced Men Are Not the Enemy — They Are Our Greatest Supporters

Many women blame men for their struggles in business and success — but this is a dangerous distortion.

The truth is that balanced, confident, and successful men are:

- Incredibly supportive of women's success
- Natural protectors and champions of balanced women
- Proud to see women rise and step into leadership
- Deeply collaborative, not competitive, with powerful women

The problem is not men — it is distorted masculine energy and distorted feminine energy in both men and women.

A millionairess does not view men as competitors — she sees them as allies.

Instead of resisting masculine energy, learn from the men who lead with integrity, confidence, and structure.

Integrate the Strength of Both Energies

If you want to succeed without burning out or feeling lost, you must activate the best of both energies within yourself.

Use masculine energy to:

- Take action with clarity and confidence
- Set boundaries and protect your time
- Create structure, goals, and long-term strategy

Use feminine energy to:

- Trust your intuition and inner knowing
- Allow opportunities to flow instead of forcing them
- Connect, inspire, and build relationships that fuel success

You do not have to be either soft or strong — you can be both.

A millionairess embodies both grace and power, intuition and strategy, flow and focus.

Stop Resisting Healthy Masculine Energy

- Some women reject masculine structure, leadership, and power because they associate it with oppression.
- But rejecting masculine energy leads to confusion, disorganization, and lack of financial clarity.

Structure and focus are not limitations — they are the foundations of freedom.

A millionairess does not fear masculine energy — she integrates it into her leadership.

Fast-Track Millionairess

Instead of rejecting structured business models, pricing strategies, and financial systems, embrace them as the tools that create sustainable wealth.

Call Out Distorted Feminine Energy in Yourself and Others

Distorted feminine energy shows up as victimhood, passivity, and resentment toward those who are succeeding.

Many women struggle because they:

- Blame external circumstances for their financial struggles instead of taking ownership.
- Expect success to "manifest" without strategy, effort, or execution.
- Wait for someone else to "save" them instead of learning financial mastery.

True feminine power is not passive — it is creative, magnetic, and transformational.

A millionairess does not sit and hope for success — she creates it while remaining open to aligned opportunities.

Surround Yourself with Balanced People

Unsuccessful people exist in both distorted masculine and feminine energy. But truly successful, powerful, and wealthy people — both men and women — have learned how to integrate balance.

To rise, you must:

- Surround yourself with men and women who embody balance.
- Learn from men who lead with integrity, vision, and strength.
- Align with women who uplift, support, and inspire instead of competing.

Your environment shapes your identity — choose it wisely.

Fast-Track Millionairess

A millionairess does not fight the wrong battles — she aligns with the right people and moves forward with clarity.

The *Fast-Track Millionairess* Power Formula

- **Your power comes** from balance, not extremes.
- **You do not have to choose between intuition and strategy** — you can embody both.
- **Men are not your enemy** — healthy masculine energy is a key to success.
- **Resisting structure and financial systems** will keep you stuck — embrace them as freedom tools.
- **Do not fall into victimhood or waiting** — take ownership of your wealth and success.
- **Surround yourself with people who embody balance** — because that is where true power exists.

Success is not about fighting against the masculine or overindulging in the feminine — it is about creating a powerful fusion of both.

A millionairess leads with wisdom, confidence, and impact — by integrating the best of both worlds.

How to Lead from A Place of Alignment Rather Than Force

For centuries, leadership has been taught as a game of force, control, and relentless hustle.

But true power — the kind that creates wealth, impact, and lasting success — comes from alignment, not exhaustion.

Aligned leadership is the difference between working hard and working in flow. It is the difference between chasing success and magnetizing it.

A millionairess does not force — she aligns, she decides, and success follows.

The Problem with Force-Based Leadership

Force-based leadership is built on pressure, control, and pushing against resistance.

Women who operate from this place:

- Overwork themselves trying to "prove" they deserve success.
- Push through resistance instead of adjusting and pivoting.
- Ignore their own exhaustion, leading to burnout.
- Cling to plans that are no longer working instead of trusting evolution.

Success is not meant to be a constant battle — it is meant to be a natural extension of who you are.

A millionairess does not chase — she aligns and allows success to unfold in her favor.

What Does It Mean to Lead from Alignment?

Alignment is when your work, energy, and purpose are in flow with each other.

When you are aligned:

- Opportunities feel natural instead of forced.
- Decisions are made with clarity, not fear.
- Your energy fuels your success instead of draining it.
- Money, clients, and results come with ease — not through struggle.

You are not here to fight your way to success — you are here to align with it.

A millionairess creates her path from a place of power, not pressure.

Fast-Track Millionairess

Lead from Vision, Not Just Strategy

Strategy without vision leads to empty success — goals that look good on paper but feel unfulfilling.

To lead with alignment, ask yourself:

- What kind of business, lifestyle, and impact do I truly want?
- Does this path excite me, or am I forcing it out of obligation?
- Am I building what I love, or what I think I "should" be doing?

If your work does not feel aligned, you are not leading — you are forcing.

A millionairess leads from deep inner knowing, not external expectations.

Follow Expansion, Not Fear

Fear-based decisions keep women stuck in survival mode.

Aligned decisions feel expansive — even if they are a little scary.

Instead of asking: *What is the safest decision?*

Ask: *What decision expands me, excites me, and aligns with my highest self?*

If it feels heavy, draining, or like you are forcing it, it is not alignment — it is resistance.

A millionairess leads by following what expands her, not what traps her.

Trust Timing and Energy, Not Just Hustle

Success is not just about working harder — it is about working in the right energy at the right time.

- If you are constantly exhausted, it is a sign to adjust — not push harder.

- If something keeps feeling blocked, step back and find a new path.
- If a door closes, trust that a better one is opening.

Hustle will never replace alignment. When you work with energy, you achieve more with less effort.

A millionairess does not force doors open — she flows through the ones meant for her.

Let Go of What No Longer Feels Right

Many women stay in situations that no longer serve them out of fear, guilt, or attachment.

- Holding onto outdated strategies, offers, or business models just because they "used to work."
- Keeping challenging relationships or partnerships out of obligation.
- Fearing change, even when growth is calling.

Alignment requires letting go of what is misaligned — so something better can take its place.

A millionairess does not cling — she evolves, expands, and allows transformation.

Make Space for Opportunities to Flow

Many women block success because they fill their time, energy, and business with unnecessary effort.

- Create space for new ideas, new strategies, and new connections.
- Do not fear stillness — clarity comes when you are not drowning in busyness.
- Trust that success does not require nonstop action — it requires intentional, high-impact moves.

Fast-Track Millionairess

Opportunities flow when you are open to receiving — not when you are forcing.

A millionairess creates space for her next level, instead of filling every moment with noise.

Be Magnetic, Not Just Productive

Most people think success is about doing more — but aligned success is about being magnetic.

- Your energy attracts the right opportunities, people, and money.
- When you are aligned, people naturally want to work with you.
- You do not have to chase clients, investors, or customers — because they are drawn to you.

Magnetism happens when you are fully aligned with what you do, who you serve, and how you lead.

A millionairess does not beg for success — she becomes the kind of leader success flows to effortlessly.

The *Fast-Track Millionairess* Alignment Formula

- **Success is not about forcing** — it is about aligning with what is meant for you.
- **Lead from vision, not just strategy** — your energy is your greatest guide.
- **Make decisions that expand you**, not ones based on fear.
- **Stop working against resistance** — flow with energy and timing.
- **Let go of what no longer serves you** — so something better can take its place.
- **Success does not come from endless hustle** — it comes from being magnetic and intentional.

You do not have to push, force, or struggle to succeed. You only have to align, lead with clarity, and trust that what is meant for you will always flow in your direction.

A millionairess leads from alignment, not exhaustion — because she knows that ease, flow, and wealth go hand in hand.

Building A Support Network of High-Vibration Men and Women

The most successful women do not rise alone — they cultivate powerful, high-vibration connections that elevate, empower, and expand them.

A millionairess does not waste time in low-energy circles. She surrounds herself with people who uplift, inspire, and challenge her to grow.

Your network is either pulling you up or holding you back — choose wisely.

Why Your Inner Circle Impacts Your Success

If you are surrounded by negativity, jealousy, or small thinking, it will drain your energy and slow your progress.

But if you are surrounded by ambitious, high-energy, success-driven people, you will accelerate beyond what you thought possible.

Your environment directly affects:

- Your mindset and confidence — The conversations you hear shape your beliefs.
- Your financial growth — Wealthy, high-level thinkers inspire you to reach new heights.
- Your emotional and spiritual well-being — Supportive relationships strengthen your energy.

You cannot become a millionairess in an environment that encourages playing small.

A millionairess cultivates a circle that matches her vision, not her fears.

Fast-Track Millionairess

Audit Your Current Circle

Take a hard look at the people around you. Ask yourself:

- Who drains my energy instead of fueling it?
- Who makes me doubt myself, shrink, or feel small?
- Who constantly complains but never takes action?
- Who subtly undermines or resents my success?

Now ask:

- Who challenges me to think bigger?
- Who supports my vision without jealousy or fear?
- Who is already at the level I want to be?
- Who truly celebrates my wins without comparison?

Your inner circle should reflect where you are going, not where you have been.

A millionairess does not hold onto relationships out of guilt — she aligns with those who elevate her energy.

Cultivate Relationships with High-Vibration Women

Not all women support each other — many operate from competition, comparison, and jealousy.

But high-vibration women uplift, inspire, and empower one another.

The right women:

- Cheer for you even when they are struggling.
- Share resources, insights, and opportunities without fear.
- Know that another woman's success does not diminish their own.
- Support you in business, wealth, and personal growth.

Fast-Track Millionairess

A true millionairess does not compete — she collaborates, she shares, and she builds with other powerful women.

Surround yourself with women who rise with you, not against you.

Align with Balanced, High-Level Men

Some women avoid working with men because they assume they will not be supportive — but this is false.

Balanced, high-caliber men are some of the biggest champions of successful women.

The right men:

- Respect and uplift ambitious women.
- Offer powerful business insights without ego or competition.
- Provide structured, logical, high-level thinking that balances feminine intuition.
- Are secure in themselves and do not feel threatened by female success.

Your greatest allies may come from men who fully support your expansion.

A millionairess does not push men away — she aligns with those who honor her power.

Seek Out Expansive Mentors and Coaches

If you only surround yourself with people at your current level, your growth will be limited.

Mentors and coaches accelerate your expansion.
Find people who have already built what you want to create.
Invest in learning from those ahead of you.
Let go of ego and be willing to receive guidance.

Fast-Track Millionairess

Success leaves clues — surround yourself with those who have walked the path before you.

A millionairess does not try to do everything alone — she seeks wisdom, applies it, and rises faster.

Eliminate Low-Energy Conversations

Words shape reality — if the conversations in your life are rooted in scarcity, gossip, and negativity, they are poisoning your success.

- High-energy conversations are focused on solutions, expansion, and wealth.
- Avoid groups that bond over complaining and self-doubt.
- Distance yourself from people who only talk about problems, not solutions.
- Stop engaging in drama — it is a distraction from your highest potential.
- Surround yourself with people who talk about ideas, strategies, and possibilities.
- Engage in conversations about wealth, mindset, and success.
- Speak only words that uplift yourself and others.
- Your voice and the voices around you are shaping your future — choose them wisely.

A millionairess does not engage in small talk — she engages in big visions.

Be the High-Vibration Person You Want to Attract

You do not just attract high-level people — you become magnetic to them by embodying the same energy.

- Be a woman who celebrates others.
- Be a woman who shares opportunities instead of hoarding them.
- Be a woman who uplifts, inspires, and expands those around her.
- Be a woman who leads, not complains.

Fast-Track Millionairess

When you embody the energy you want to receive, the right people will naturally align with you.

A millionairess does not wait for the right circle — she becomes the kind of woman that high-level people want to be around.

The Fast-Track Millionairess Network Formula

- **Your network impacts your success** — choose it with intention.
- **Surround yourself with ambitious, high-energy women** who uplift and inspire.
- **Align with balanced, powerful men** who support female leadership.
- **Seek out mentors who challenge you** to expand beyond your current level.
- **Cut out low-energy conversations**, gossip, and negativity.
- **Be the high-vibration person** you want to attract.

You are a reflection of the people you spend the most time with — so build a circle that accelerates your wealth, success, and leadership.

A millionairess does not wait for support — she creates an empire of powerful, aligned people who rise together.

Chapter 11: The Freedom Formula — Designing a Life You Love

Creating A Business That Works for You, Not the Other Way Around

Most people start a business because they want freedom.

But instead of creating a life of ease, flexibility, and fulfillment, they build a business that:

- Consumes all their time and energy
- Requires them to work harder than they ever did in a job
- Leaves them exhausted, overwhelmed, and trapped in their own creation

A millionairess does not build a business that controls her — she builds a business that serves her.

Your business should work for you, not the other way around.

Define Your Freedom First — Then Build the Business Model Around It

Most entrepreneurs do this backwards:

They build a business first, then try to "fit" freedom into it later.

The right way?

Decide what kind of life you want first — then create a business model that aligns with it.

Ask yourself:

- How many hours a week do I actually want to work?
- What kind of daily lifestyle do I want?

Fast-Track Millionairess

- *Do I want location freedom? Time freedom? Creative freedom?*
- *Do I want to work with clients 1:1, or do I want scalable, automated income?*

If your business does not support your desired life, you have built the wrong business model.

A millionairess designs her business around her life — not the other way around.

Stop Trading Time for Money — Leverage Scalable Income Streams

If your business only makes money when you work, you do not own a business — you own a job.

To create freedom, your income must be:

- Scalable — So your earning potential is not limited by your hours.
- Predictable — So you are not constantly chasing new clients.
- Automated — So money flows in even when you are not working.

Smart businesswomen do not just make money — they build systems that make money for them.

A millionairess does not trade her hours for income — she builds wealth on autopilot.

Choose Business Models That Align with Freedom

To create a business that works for you, choose income models that support freedom.

Scalable Income Models:

- Digital Courses — Teach once, sell forever.
- Memberships and Subscriptions — Recurring income without chasing clients.

Fast-Track Millionairess

- Passive Income Products — E-books, templates, programs that sell 24/7.
- Affiliate Marketing — Earn money recommending what you love.
- YouTube or Content Monetization — Build an audience, get paid while you sleep.

You do not need to work harder — you need to work smarter.

A millionairess builds income streams that make money with or without her presence.

Set Boundaries That Protect Your Freedom

A business without boundaries will consume your life.

To maintain freedom:

- Set clear work hours — and stick to them.
- Create structured offers — no custom work that drains you.
- Say NO to misaligned clients, projects, and distractions.
- Automate, delegate, and outsource anything that is not your zone of genius.

Freedom is not given — it is designed through boundaries and business systems.

A millionairess does not let clients, work, or obligations control her time — she builds her business on her terms.

Eliminate Overcomplication — Keep Business Simple and Profitable

Many women build businesses that are far too complicated — more work, more stress, less money.

Instead:

- Streamline offers — fewer, high-value services/products instead of endless options.

Fast-Track Millionairess

- Automate everything possible — emails, payments, onboarding, client communication.
- Use systems to free up time — tech tools, scheduling apps, outsourcing.

The more you simplify, the more profitable and enjoyable your business becomes.

A millionairess creates maximum impact with minimum effort — she does not overcomplicate success.

Make Decisions Like a CEO, Not an Employee

Employees think about tasks. Millionairesses think about leverage.

Instead of asking:

- *How can I get more clients?*
- *How can I work harder to earn more?*

Ask:

- *How can I create value that sells itself?*
- *How can I scale my income without adding more hours?*
- *How can I replace myself in the business while it keeps growing?*

Freedom happens when you stop thinking like a worker and start thinking like a visionary leader.

A millionairess does not grind — she builds smart, scalable systems that allow her to live freely.

Design a Life That Matches Your Wealth

Some women build successful businesses but forget to actually enjoy their wealth.

- Do not just create financial freedom — create lifestyle freedom.
- Do not work harder for more money — work smarter for more time.

- Do not let your business be the thing that steals your joy — make it the thing that fuels it.

Your business should give you more time for the things you love — not take it all away.

A millionairess is not just rich — she is free, fulfilled, and fully in control of her life.

The *Fast-Track Millionairess* Freedom Formula

- **Design your business around your life** — not the other way around.
- **Stop trading time for money** — build scalable, automated income.
- **Choose business models** that give you freedom, not exhaustion.
- **Set boundaries so your business** supports you instead of draining you.
- **Simplify** — complexity does not equal success.
- **Think like a CEO, not an employee** — focus on leverage, not tasks.
- **Create a life you actually love** — money is meaningless if you have no time to enjoy it.

You did not build your business to become a slave to it. You built it to create freedom, wealth, and impact on YOUR terms.

A millionairess does not let her business run her — she builds a business that works for her, giving her the life she truly desires.

Wealth as A Tool for Personal Freedom and Global Impact

Many women hesitate to fully embrace wealth because they have been conditioned to believe:

- Money is selfish.
- Wanting wealth makes you materialistic.
- Having more means taking from others.

None of this is true. Money does not corrupt — it amplifies who you already are.

Fast-Track Millionairess

A millionairess understands that wealth is not just personal gain — it is a tool for freedom, empowerment, and global change.

Redefine Wealth as a Form of Power and Choice

Many women chase money without understanding its real purpose — FREEDOM.

Wealth is not just about:

- Buying luxury things
- Looking successful
- Keeping up with others

Real wealth is about:

- Freedom of time — You decide how you spend your days.
- Freedom of location — You are not tied to one place.
- Freedom of choice — You do not make decisions based on financial limitations.
- Freedom to give — You can impact causes, people, and communities.

Money is not about greed — it is about control over your own destiny.

A millionairess does not chase money — she wields it as a tool for her highest vision.

Use Wealth to Create a Life of Expansion

Wealth is not the goal — what you do with it is.

Once you have financial freedom, you can:

- Travel and experience the world.
- Take care of your health without limitations.
- Surround yourself with inspiring, high-vibration people.
- Spend your time on passion projects, creativity, and purpose-driven work.

Fast-Track Millionairess

Money should not trap you — it should expand you.

A millionairess does not work for money — she makes money work for her, creating a life of limitless possibilities.

Use Wealth to Elevate Others

Many women feel guilty about making money because they think it is selfish.

But wealth allows you to help others at a higher level.

With financial power, you can:

- Support your family without stress.
- Invest in businesses, education, and mentorship for others.
- Create opportunities for people who lack them.
- Fund charities and movements that create real change.

You cannot help others if you are struggling yourself. Wealth allows you to give from a place of strength, not sacrifice.

A millionairess does not just build wealth for herself — she uses it to uplift others.

Become a Conscious Wealth Creator

Money in the hands of conscious, empowered women changes the world.

When women control wealth:

- Communities thrive.
- Education improves.
- Families break cycles of struggle.
- Businesses are built with heart, integrity, and impact.

You are not just making money for yourself — you are creating a ripple effect that changes lives.

Fast-Track Millionairess

A millionairess is not afraid of money — she masters it, multiplies it, and uses it for impact.

Think Beyond Personal Success — Build a Legacy

Real wealth is about more than just today — it is about lasting impact.

Ask yourself:

- What do I want my financial legacy to be?
- How can I use my wealth to empower future generations?
- How can I create lasting impact in my community and the world?

True wealth is not just about making money — it is about what you leave behind.

A millionairess does not think small — she builds a legacy that lasts beyond her lifetime.

The *Fast-Track Millionairess* Wealth Formula

- **Wealth is not just about luxury** — it is about freedom and choice.
- **Money is not the end goal** — it is the tool that allows you to create the life you desire.
- **You cannot help others if you are struggling** — financial power allows you to give at a higher level.
- **When women build wealth**, they change their families, communities, and the world.
- **Wealth is not about accumulating** — it is about creating a lasting impact.

You are not here to struggle — you are here to thrive, to lead, and to change lives through wealth, freedom, and purpose.

A millionairess does not just make money — she creates a legacy of power, impact, and transformation.

Committing to Your Future One Self-Supportive Step at A Time

The journey to wealth, freedom, and success is not about one huge, life-changing moment — it is about a series of small, intentional, self-supportive choices made every day.

A millionairess is not created overnight — she is built through consistent, aligned action.

Every decision you make either moves you closer to your vision or keeps you stuck where you are. The choice is always yours.

Stop Waiting for the "Right Time"

There is no perfect moment to start. No magical time when all conditions are ideal.

- If you are waiting for more money, more confidence, more clarity — you will wait forever.
- The only way to create your future is to begin, adjust, and keep going.
- The fastest way to succeed is to start before you feel ready.

A millionairess does not wait — she takes action now and figures things out as she moves.

Make Your Future Self Proud

Every choice you make today shapes the woman you are becoming.

Ask yourself:

- *What decision will my future self thank me for?*
- *What small step today will create momentum for tomorrow?*
- *What is one thing I can commit to that moves me forward?*

Fast-Track Millionairess

Growth happens in daily steps, not giant leaps. Keep moving forward, even if it feels slow.

A millionairess builds her future with every choice she makes today.

Replace Self-Doubt with Self-Support

The biggest reason women stay stuck? They do not support themselves — they talk themselves out of their own success.

- They question whether they are "good enough."
- They wait for external validation before trusting themselves.
- They sabotage opportunities by playing small.

A millionairess does the opposite:

- She backs herself fully, even when no one else does.
- She takes risks because she knows she can handle the outcome.
- She believes in her vision, even before it becomes reality.

You will only go as far as your self-belief allows. Choose to believe in yourself now — not later.

A millionairess does not wait for confidence — she builds it by taking action.

Commit to Growth, Not Perfection

Perfectionism kills progress.

- If you wait for everything to be "perfect," you will never move forward.
- If you try to avoid mistakes, you will never take the risks necessary for success.

The goal is not perfection — the goal is momentum.

- Start before you are ready.

- Learn as you go.
- Embrace mistakes as part of the process.

Every successful woman was once a beginner who took messy, imperfect action.

A millionairess does not fear mistakes — she uses them as stepping-stones to mastery.

Build Self-Supportive Habits Daily

Success is not about one grand decision — it is about daily habits that align with your future vision.

- Track your financial goals — daily, weekly, monthly.
- Invest time in learning, growing, and refining your skills.
- Prioritize self-care — because a burnt-out woman cannot lead.
- Surround yourself with people who elevate your thinking.

You do not have to get everything right today — just take one step that moves you forward.

A millionairess builds habits that support her success every single day.

Stay Committed, Even When It Feels Hard

There will be days when you feel tired, discouraged, or uncertain.

Your success is determined not by how you feel in the moment, but by how you continue despite those feelings.

The women who make it are not the ones who never struggle — they are the ones who never quit.

The key to success? Stay committed, no matter what.

- Keep showing up.

- Keep taking the next step.
- Keep believing in yourself, even when no one else does.

The only way to fail is to stop trying.

A millionairess does not give up — she adapts, she learns, and she keeps going.

The Fast-Track Millionairess Commitment Formula

- **There is no perfect time to start** — take action now.
- **Every decision you make today** shapes your future self.
- **Stop waiting for confidence** — build it through action.
- **Perfection is not required** — momentum is.
- **Daily habits create long-term success** — stay consistent.
- **Commit to your vision,** even when no one else can see it yet.

You are not here to wish for success — you are here to create it, step by step, with full self-support.

A millionairess does not wait, hesitate, or overthink — she commits, moves forward, and becomes unstoppable.

The Fast-Track Millionairess Action Plan

You now have the mindset, the strategies, and the roadmap to create wealth, freedom, and impact on your terms.

- But knowledge alone is not enough.
- Nothing changes unless you take action.

A millionairess is not just someone who dreams of success — she commits, executes, and moves forward relentlessly.

Here's your step-by-step action plan to implement everything you have learned and start creating real, tangible results.

Fast-Track Millionairess

Commit to a Millionaire-Level Mindset

If you do not control your thoughts, your thoughts will control your wealth.

- Rewire limiting beliefs about money, success, and self-worth.
- Eliminate scarcity thinking — start operating from abundance.
- Refuse to play small — expand your vision of what is possible.

Your business, income, and success will never grow beyond your mindset.

A millionairess thinks like a wealthy woman before she becomes one.

Design a Business That Works for You

Your business should give you freedom — not trap you in endless work.

- Choose a business model that aligns with your desired lifestyle.
- Set clear income goals — and design scalable offers to reach them.
- Stop trading time for money — focus on leverage, automation, and passive income.

A millionairess builds a business that creates wealth, time, and impact — not just work.

If your business does not give you the life you want, change the model.

Set Boundaries That Protect Your Time and Energy

Without boundaries, success turns into exhaustion.

- Say NO to misaligned opportunities, clients, and distractions.
- Automate, delegate, and outsource everything outside your zone of genius.
- Prioritize your well-being — because burnout is not part of the plan.

Success is sustainable only when it supports your energy, not drains it.

Fast-Track Millionairess

A millionairess does not let others dictate her schedule — she sets the rules.

Master Financial Growth and Wealth Building

You cannot be a millionairess if you avoid money.

- Take full ownership of your finances — track income, expenses, and growth.
- Invest in scalable income streams — digital products, courses, real estate, stocks.
- Eliminate unnecessary debt — free your money to work for you.

Your financial future is in your hands — command it with confidence.

A millionairess does not just make money — she grows and multiplies it.

Build a High-Vibration Support Network

Your environment impacts how far you will go.

- Surround yourself with successful, high-energy, expansive thinkers.
- Let go of people who drain your energy or limit your vision.
- Align with mentors, coaches, and communities that accelerate your success.

Success is not an easy journey — choose your circle wisely.

A millionairess surrounds herself with people who inspire, challenge, and uplift her.

Develop an Action-Taking Habit

Ideas are worthless without execution.

- Take bold action daily — progress matters more than perfection.
- Make fast decisions — overthinking kills momentum.

Fast-Track Millionairess

- Support yourself — confidence comes from action, not waiting.
- Trust your intuition — it's your *Fast Track Millionairess* super-power

Success does not happen by waiting — it happens by doing.

A millionairess moves forward, even when the path is uncertain.

Show Up Consistently — No Matter What

The only difference between those who succeed and those who don't? Commitment.

- Stay disciplined — take action even when motivation fades.
- Refuse to quit — adjust, adapt, but never stop moving forward.
- Keep your vision clear — remind yourself daily why you are doing this.

Success is not about luck — it is about showing up, day after day, no matter what.

A millionairess does not hope for success — she makes it inevitable.

The *Fast-Track Millionairess* Success Formula

- **Your mindset determines your wealth** — reprogram it for success.
- **Your business should give you freedom** — if it doesn't, redesign it.
- **Boundaries protect your success** — set them and enforce them.
- **Wealth is not just made** — it is grown, multiplied, and protected.
- **Your circle either lifts you or limits you** — choose people who elevate you.
- **Action creates momentum** — execute boldly, refine as you go.
- **Consistency is everything** — keep showing up until success is undeniable.
- **Patience is necessary** — business growth is not a linear process
- **Trust your gut** — your intuition will never let you down.

You do not have to be the smartest, the most talented, or the most experienced — you just have to be the one who commits, takes action, and refuses to stop.

Fast-Track Millionairess

A millionairess does not wait for success — she creates it, step by step, with unshakable belief and relentless execution.

Your Next Move: Take the First Step NOW

You now have everything you need to create wealth, impact, and freedom. The only thing left? Take action.

- Decide what your first step will be — right now.
- Commit to doing something today that moves you forward.
- Trust that success is already yours — it is just waiting for you to claim it.

Your millionairess journey starts now. Are you ready?

Let's go. The future is waiting for you to rise.

Conclusion: Becoming the Wealthy Woman You Were Born to Be

A Final Mindset Shift for Lasting Success

You now have the tools, the strategies, and the roadmap to create wealth, freedom, and power on your own terms.

But the most important shift of all?

Deciding, once and for all, that you are worthy of the life you desire.

Because the only thing standing between you and success is your willingness to step into it.

The Old Mindset Vs. The Millionairess Mindset

The old you:

- Hesitated, doubted, and questioned her worth.
- Waited for the "right time" or external validation.
- Played small to make others comfortable.
- Feared judgment, failure, or outshining others.
- Believed that money and success were hard to achieve.

The millionairess you:

- Moves forward with confidence, no matter what.
- Acts now instead of waiting for the perfect moment.
- Takes up space unapologetically.
- Embraces success without guilt, fear, or hesitation.
- Understands that wealth is a tool for freedom, impact, and joy.

Fast-Track Millionairess

The only thing that ever kept you from success was the belief that you weren't ready.

But you are ready. You always were. And now, you claim it.

Own Your Wealth Without Apology

Women are conditioned to feel guilty about money, power, and ambition.

But the world needs more wealthy women who lead with wisdom, heart, and purpose.

- You are allowed to want more.
- You are allowed to be rich, successful, and powerful.
- You are allowed to build a life that others only dream of.

Your wealth does not take from anyone — it expands what is possible for everyone.

A millionairess does not seek permission to succeed — she steps into it boldly.

Stop Looking Back — Your Future is Calling

You cannot create your next level of success while holding onto your past limitations.

- Let go of past failures.
- Let go of old stories about money and success.
- Let go of doubts, fears, and what others think.

Turn fully toward your future. Step forward, and never look back.

Your past does not define you — your next move does.

A millionairess is always future-focused, walking with certainty into the life she is creating.

Fast-Track Millionairess

Choose Growth Over Comfort — Every Single Time

Everything you desire is on the other side of the discomfort you have been avoiding.

- If you want more money, you must face your fears around wealth.
- If you want more freedom, you must let go of control.
- If you want more success, you must be willing to be seen.

Your comfort zone is the prison of your potential — step beyond it.

A millionairess does not wait until she feels "ready" — she grows into her success by taking action now.

Embody the Wealthy Woman Today — Not "Someday"

You do not "become" a millionairess when you have the money — you become her first, and the wealth follows.

- Act, think, and move like the woman who already has it.
- Make decisions from your future self, not your fears.
- Invest in yourself and your growth — because you are your greatest asset.
- Carry yourself like the powerful, successful woman you are becoming.

Wealth, success, and confidence are not destinations — they are choices you make now.

A millionairess steps into her identity today, and the world rises to meet her.

The *Fast-Track Millionairess* Mindset Formula

- **You are already worthy** of wealth, success, and freedom.
- **Your past does not define you** — your next step does.
- **Growth is always outside your comfort zone** — lean into it.

- **You become wealthy** by thinking, acting, and moving like a millionairess now.
- **Your time is now** — not someday, not later — now.

You are not waiting for success — you are claiming it, stepping into it, and living it, starting today.

A millionairess does not hope, wish, or wait — she decides, she acts, and she rises.

This is your moment.

This is your time.

The world is waiting for you to step into your power.

Are you ready? Then go. The millionairess version of you is already here — step into her fully, and never look back.

Encouragement to Take Action Now

Everything you need to create wealth, freedom, and success is already within you.

You have read the strategies. You have the mindset shifts. You understand the path.

But none of it matters unless you take action.

Success is not for the smartest, the luckiest, or the most talented — it is for the ones who are willing to move, right now, without hesitation.

A millionairess does not wait for the "perfect moment" to begin — she starts where she is and builds from there.

The Only Difference Between Those Who Succeed and Those Who Don't

The people who never reach their goals?

Fast-Track Millionairess

- They read, plan, and research — but never take real action.
- They wait for clarity instead of creating it through movement.
- They let fear stop them instead of pushing forward despite it.

The people who become millionairesses?

- They start before they feel ready.
- They make decisions and trust themselves to adjust as they go.
- They act now, knowing that momentum is the key to success.

The only thing standing between you and the life you want is the decision to go for it.

A millionairess does not hesitate — she chooses, she commits, and she moves.

Decide That You Are Ready — Because You Are

If you are waiting for some magical moment where everything feels "ready," you will wait forever.

You do not need to feel fully confident — you need to be willing to move forward despite the uncertainty.

- Decide that now is your time.
- Decide that you are capable, powerful, and worthy of success.
- Decide that you will no longer wait, hesitate, or overthink.

Your future begins the moment you decide to claim it.

A millionairess does not wait for confidence — she builds it by taking action.

Take One Step Right Now

Do not just think about it. Do not just plan. Do something — now.

Your next move depends on where you are in your journey:

Fast-Track Millionairess

- Starting a business? Register the domain, create the first product, launch the first offer.
- Growing wealth? Open the investment account, automate savings, track your finances.
- Shifting your mindset? Write down your new success beliefs, start the daily affirmations, rewire your money story.
- Big change starts with one small action. Take the step, and momentum will follow.

A millionairess moves even when she does not know the full path — because movement creates clarity.

Expect Success and Adjust as You Go

Perfectionism is the enemy of action.

You do not need to have everything figured out — you just need to begin.

- Trust that the answers will come as you move.
- Know that every decision can be adjusted and improved along the way.
- Stay focused on progress, not perfection.

There is no such thing as failure — only learning, refining, and moving forward.

A millionairess does not need all the answers before she starts — she figures them out along the way.

Commit to Staying in Motion

Many people start — but very few stay committed long enough to see the results.

Your success is guaranteed if you refuse to quit.

- Take consistent action, no matter what.
- Push forward even when motivation fades.

- Remember: Every successful woman was once where you are now — but she KEPT GOING.

You do not need to be perfect — you just need to be relentless.

A millionairess does not stop when it gets hard — she adapts, adjusts, and keeps moving forward.

The *Fast-Track Millionairess* Action Formula

- **Success is not about knowing everything** — it is about taking action before you feel ready.
- **Decide that NOW is your time** — because waiting is a waste of your potential.
- **Take one step today** — momentum comes from movement.
- **Perfection is not required** — progress is.
- **Stay committed** — your future is built by your daily actions.

Your millionairess journey begins NOW, with the action you take today. Not tomorrow. Not next week. NOW.

So take the step. The path is waiting for you to walk it.

Are you ready? Then go. The world is waiting for you to rise.

The Next Steps for Readers

You've made it to the final pages of this book — but this is not the end.

This is the beginning of your next-level life, wealth, and success.

Everything you need to become the millionairess version of yourself is already in your hands. The only thing left?

Take the next steps. Take action. Move forward — right now.

Fast-Track Millionairess

Commit to Your Next Level — Fully and Completely

Nothing changes until you make the decision to step into your next level of success.

Right now, declare:

- I am ready to create my next level of success.
- I am done with waiting, doubting, and playing small.
- I am stepping fully into my millionairess identity — starting today.

Success is a decision before it becomes a reality. Make the decision now.

A millionairess does not "hope" — she decides, she commits, and she follows through.

Take Immediate Action — Right Now

Action creates momentum. Thinking about action does nothing.

Ask yourself:

- What is one thing I can do TODAY to move forward?
- What is one decision I have been delaying that I can make now?
- What is one financial, business, or mindset action I can take immediately?

DO IT. Right now. No waiting. No excuses.

Your next level is waiting — but only if you are willing to step into it.

A millionairess does not wait for motivation — she creates momentum through action.

Implement the Millionairess Strategies in Your Life and Business

Re-read the key sections of this book and apply them step by step.

Fast-Track Millionairess

- Mindset: Shift your beliefs around money, success, and self-worth.
- Business: Build scalable income, stop trading time for money, and create systems for freedom.
- Wealth: Master financial growth, investments, and cash flow.
- Energy: Balance action with alignment, set boundaries, and work with your natural rhythms.
- Success Habits: Show up daily, take bold action, and stay committed to the long game.

You do not have to implement everything at once — just start somewhere and build from there.

A millionairess is not overwhelmed by success — she takes it step by step and keeps moving forward.

Surround Yourself with High-Vibration People

Your environment will either accelerate or sabotage your success.

- Align with other ambitious, driven, successful women.
- Find mentors, coaches, or networks that push you to grow.
- Remove yourself from negative, small-minded conversations.

You are a product of the people you spend time with — choose your circle wisely.

A millionairess builds her empire with people who inspire, uplift, and challenge her to rise higher.

Get the Guidance and Support You Need

If you are serious about taking action, then you need a clear, step-by-step framework to follow.

That's exactly why I created my signature course: **Create Your Freedom.**

Fast-Track Millionairess

- It's designed for women like you — ambitious, driven, and ready to build wealth on their own terms.
- It walks you through the exact process of designing a business that gives you financial and personal freedom.
- It helps you build a sustainable, scalable income while staying aligned with your energy and values.

You do not have to figure this out alone — there is a proven path to creating financial success on your terms.

A millionairess does not waste time trying to "guess" her way to success — she follows a clear, powerful system and executes.

Stay in Motion — No Matter What

The only way to fail is to stop moving.

- There will be challenges — push through them.
- There will be moments of doubt — trust yourself anyway.
- There will be days when it feels hard — keep going.

Success is not about never struggling — it is about never stopping.

A millionairess does not quit — she adapts, she learns, and she keeps rising.

Step Fully into Your Millionairess Identity

This is not just about making money — it is about becoming the woman you were born to be.

- Lead with confidence.
- Charge what you are worth.
- Own your success unapologetically.
- Embody the version of yourself who already has everything she desires.

Fast-Track Millionairess

You are not waiting for wealth — you are stepping into it.

A millionairess does not wait to become successful — she lives as her highest self now, and the world adjusts to her energy.

The *Fast-Track Millionairess* Next Steps Formula

- **Decide that NOW is your time** — no more waiting.
- **Take immediate action** — momentum comes from movement.
- **Apply what you've learned** — knowledge without action is wasted.
- **Align with powerful, high-vibration people** — your circle determines your growth.
- **Join Create Your Freedom** for expert guidance and a proven success framework.
- **Stay in motion** — consistency is the key to success.
- **Embody your millionairess identity** — live it before you "arrive."

This is your moment. Everything you desire is within reach — but only if you step up and claim it.

You are not here to play small. You are here to rise, to lead, and to create massive wealth, freedom, and impact.

So go. Take the step. Your millionairess future is waiting for you to walk into it.

The Create Your Freedom Course

You've read the strategies. You've shifted your mindset. You know what's possible.

Now, it's time to turn your knowledge into reality.

Your millionairess journey doesn't stop here — this is just the beginning.

And I am here to help you take the next steps with full clarity, confidence, and a proven success path.

Turn Your Passion into a Thriving Online Business and Grow Your Own Soul-Aligned Community

Are you ready to transform your expertise, passion, or creativity into a thriving 6- or 7-figure online business?

This is your chance to stop dreaming and start building.

My comprehensive Create Your Freedom course will take you from where you are now to a profitable, soul-aligned business and community in just one year.

No prior experience? No problem. This course meets you exactly where you are and gives you the step-by-step framework to grow, scale, and thrive.

What You'll Learn in This Course

Chart Your Course: Align your long-term business vision with your energy and soul's purpose.

Overcome Fear and Limiting Beliefs: Crush imposter syndrome and confidently own your expertise.

Fast-Track Millionairess

Master Financial Confidence: Plan your cash flow, pricing, and financial strategy like a pro.

Unlock Your Intuition for Business: Use inner guidance for smarter, aligned decision-making.

Build Your Own YouTube Channel: Connect with your ideal audience and grow your visibility.

Create Content Smarter, Not Harder: Develop a content strategy that attracts and engages.

Design a Website That Sells: Showcase your brand, accept payments, and automate sales.

Set the Right Prices: Attract the right customers with strategic, value-based pricing.

Grow and Nurture a Community: Build a loyal, engaged audience while maintaining boundaries.

Balance Business and Life: Keep your energy aligned for sustainable success.

Master Bookkeeping and Financial Tools: Learn how to use Xero and track your income like a CEO.

Achieve Scalable Growth: Implement systems for long-term, sustainable expansion.

This isn't just another business course. It's a *transformational experience* that aligns your energy, intuition, and strategy for wealth and impact.

6 Months of Live Coaching and Exclusive Community Access

You don't have to do this alone. I'll be there to guide you every step of the way.

Fast-Track Millionairess

Monthly 2-Hour Live Business Coaching: Join me live for deep-dive coaching sessions where I'll cover popular business topics, answer your questions, and help you overcome obstacles in real time.

Exclusive Islay Wellness Entrepreneurs and Creatives Club: Gain instant access to my private support community — a soul-aligned network of entrepreneurs, creatives, and visionaries all building their dreams together.

This is your chance to build a business that fuels your freedom, impact, and wealth — on your terms.

Are you ready?

Scan here to Fast-Track YOUR Success and Create YOUR Freedom.

Because success is much easier when you have the right support to guide you.

Join the Islay Wellness Entrepreneurs & Creatives Club

Wealth. Success. Freedom. Community.

Success isn't just about what you know—it's about who you surround yourself with. If you're ready to take your journey even further, then The Islay Wellness Entrepreneurs & Creatives Club is the perfect place to grow, connect, and build alongside other ambitious, like-minded women.

What is the Club?

The Islay Wellness Entrepreneurs & Creatives Club is a thriving community designed for women who are building wealth, businesses, and creative ventures—without burnout.

Whether you're an entrepreneur, a creative, or simply someone who wants to step into greater freedom and abundance, this club is here to support you.

Inside the Club, You'll Get:

- Live Monthly Business and Strategy Sessions – Get expert insights and coaching to fast-track your success.
- Exclusive Member-Only Resources and Trainings – Access tools, templates, and strategies to grow your business with ease.
- A High-Vibe Network of Like-Minded Women – Surround yourself with people who get it and will uplift and inspire you.
- Direct Access to Me – Ask your burning questions, get feedback, and stay accountable.
- Early Access to New Offers and Special Discounts – Be the first to know about new programs and exclusive bonuses.

Fast-Track Millionairess

Who Can Join?

If you're part of the Create Your Freedom program—you automatically get 6 months of access to the club as part of your journey!

Not in the course? No problem! You can join the club as a standalone member and start benefiting immediately.

Scan the QR code below to find out more and join today!

Because success is even sweeter when you have the right people by your side.

Fast-Track Millionairess

The *Fast-Track Millionairess* Next Steps Formula

- **Decide that NOW is your time** — no more waiting.
- **Take immediate action** — momentum comes from movement.
- **Apply what you've learned** — knowledge without action is wasted.
- **Align with powerful, high-vibration people** — your circle impacts your growth.
- **Join *Create Your Freedom*** to get expert guidance and a proven framework.
- **Stay in motion** — consistency is the key to success.
- **Embody your millionairess identity** — live it before you "arrive."

You are not here to play small. You are here to rise, to lead, and to create massive wealth, freedom, and impact.

So take the step. Your future is waiting for you to claim it.

Let's build your millionairess empire — together.

About the Author: Heather Ogilvie

Heather is a business visionary, transformation mentor, and financial strategist who has spent her career breaking barriers, building empires, and redefining success for women.

From becoming a young female board leader in the corporate world to leading global business turnarounds, mergers, and acquisitions, Heather has been at the forefront of high-level decision-making and strategic growth. She has built, scaled, and deconstructed businesses across multiple industries, countries, and cultures, gaining an insider's perspective on what truly makes enterprises — and people — successful.

But after years at the top of the corporate world, Heather realized something profound: the system was broken.

- Success was measured in spreadsheets, not impact.
- Creativity was suffocated under layers of bureaucracy.
- The corporate world had lost its heart, its humanity, and its joy.

Most of all, she saw how women — especially ambitious, brilliant women — struggled in ways they shouldn't have to. Not because they lacked intelligence,

Fast-Track Millionairess

drive, or talent, but because they had been conditioned to undercharge, overgive, and play small.

So, Heather walked away. She built her own success — on her own terms.

She launched a thriving online business from scratch, mastering digital entrepreneurship, intuitive leadership, and wealth-building strategies that put freedom and fulfillment first. In under a year, she scaled her new business into a six-figure success, proving that financial independence doesn't have to come at the cost of burnout or sacrifice.

Now, she helps other women do the same.

As the author of **Fast-Track Millionairess** and creator of the **Create Your Freedom** program, Heather empowers women to step into their full potential, build thriving businesses, and create wealth with ease. Her work blends strategic business growth with deep mindset transformation, energy alignment, and financial mastery.

Her philosophy? Success should feel good.

Women do not need to hustle harder — they need to align smarter. Wealth is not just about making money — it's about freedom, impact, and self-worth.
You do not need permission to be powerful — you need to claim it.

Heather's mission is clear: to help women stop playing small, break free from outdated conditioning, and step into the wealth, success, and freedom they were born for.

Are you ready to become the millionairess version of yourself? Because Heather is here to show you how.

Follow Heather's work and join her programs at www.islaywellness.com.

Printed in Great Britain
by Amazon